I0037598

THE CORPORATE GIFTING PLAYBOOK

THE CORPORATE GIFTING PLAYBOOK

STRATEGIES TO BUILD LOYALTY AND DRIVE BUSINESS GROWTH THROUGH GIFTING.

DOM LEROUX

Book Disclaimer & Copyright

The information contained in this book is for general informational purposes only. The author and publisher have made every effort to ensure the accuracy of the information presented; however, they do not assume any responsibility for errors or omissions. The content is provided on an as-is basis, and readers are advised to consult professionals or experts in specific fields for specialized advice or guidance.

The author and publisher disclaim any liability for any loss or damages arising from the use or reliance on the information provided in this book. The opinions expressed in this book are solely those of the author and do not necessarily reflect the views of the publisher.

Copyright Information:

Copyright © 2024 NILDUO LLC

All rights reserved. No part of this book may be reproduced, stored in a retrieval system, or transmitted in any form or by any means, electronic, mechanical, photocopying, recording, or otherwise, without the prior written permission of the copyright owner, except for brief quotations embodied in critical reviews and certain other noncommercial uses permitted by copyright law.

For permission requests, please contact the publisher at hello@niludo.com.

ISBN: 979-8-9915620-7-2
Printed in United States
First Edition: 2024
Published by NILUDO LLC
www.niludo.com

This book is dedicated to my mother, who gave me the greatest gift—the gift of life. She did her best with what she had and what she could. She believed in me unconditionally, called me her "little resourceful go-getter," and always knew that if anyone could do it, whatever it was, she could count on me.

Reviews

"in 'The Corporate Gifting Playbook' as Dom expertly combines psychology and practicality to showcase the potential of personalized gifts for exceptional business success."

- SHAY ROWBOTTOM,
FOUNDER OF SHAY ROWBOTTOM MARKETING

"Dom masterfully explores how tailoring corporate gifts to individual recipients can create meaningful connections and leave a lasting impression."

- JAMAR JONES,
FOUNDER OF FOUREVA MEDIA

"Innovative and eye-opening. Dom's strategies will revolutionize how you approach client and employee appreciation."

- AMBER WEBER COTA/L
CERTIFIED OCCUPATIONAL THERAPY ASSISTANT, HAWAI'I STATE
DEPARTMENT OF EDUCATION

"Concise yet comprehensive. This playbook offers actionable insights to transform your corporate gifting from routine to remarkable."

- CATHY GONÇALVES, CPA
CPA AT CCMG

"Dom's insights in 'The Corporate Gifting Playbook' transform the art of gifting into a powerful strategy for building unparalleled business relationships."

- BRIAN RATLIFF
CHIEF REVENUE OFFICER AT ASSETWATCH

"The 'Corporate Gifting Playbook' revolutionizes business relationships, unveiling how strategic generosity transforms thoughtful gifts into powerful catalysts for unrivaled growth and loyalty."

- SYLVAIN ST-PIERRE,
BUSINESS DEVELOPMENT MANAGER

"The Corporate Gifting Playbook' is a game-changer. Dom LeRoux offers innovative strategies to turn gifting into a powerful tool for building client relationships and loyalty—invaluable for my Medspa business."

- KAREN DEBARON
FOUNDER OF KAREN MEDSPA

Table ofContents

Foreword

Dom LeRoux, author of "The Corporate Gifting Playbook" and a recognized expert in strategic corporate gifting, shares his insights in this essential guide.

Dom took a year-long journey, distributing his "Lucky Penny Candles" to business owners throughout the U.S. and Canada. Attending numerous events and observing the effects of his gifting strategy, he documented measurable successes that demonstrate how well-chosen gifts can boost business relationships.

This book reveals how corporate gifting can be a powerful tool for building strong connections with both employees and clients. Strategic gifts are not just thoughtful gestures—they play a critical role in attracting new clients, retaining employees, and maintaining loyalty from existing customers.

Through real-life examples, including Dom's own experiences with "Lucky Penny Candles," you will learn how effective gifting can attract new business, enhance employee morale, and secure customer loyalty.

The insights shared here will show you the psychological motivations behind corporate gifting and how understanding these can help your business. Whether it's recognizing an employee's hard work or expressing gratitude to a client, the strategic use of gifts can leave a lasting impression that contributes to the success of your business.

By exploring the "Why" and "How" of strategic gifting, this book provides a wealth of ideas and proven strategies. It equips business owners, directors, and managers with the knowledge to use gifting as a catalyst for sales growth, expanding client bases, seizing opportunities, and retaining talented employees. The practical gifting processes and methodologies outlined can be integrated into any business model, regardless of industry size or offerings.

This book will serve as your trusted guide, helping you unlock new possibilities for your business and forge lasting connections with those who matter most.

Acknowledgements

I would like to extend my heartfelt appreciation to the following individuals who have made significant contributions and provided unwavering support throughout the journey of creating this book:

Shay Rowbottom, for providing me opportunities to test, participate and measure corporate gifting strategies to help reach new prospective clients at local events and showing appreciation to current clients.

Jamar Jones, for your assistance in creating opportunities to provide corporate gifts to your customers and prospects, and for your valuable insights and creative input that have enriched the corporate gifting experience.

Debby Midkiff, for your support and encouragement all along the way. I'm deeply grateful for your unwavering belief in me and this project. Thank you for being my champion.

Aamir Khan, for your expertise and assistance, and for your meticulous editing and attention to detail, ensuring the clarity of the manuscript.

Karen DeBaron, for your encouragement and continuous belief in the project, inspiring me to persevere.

Jocelyn LeRoux, for your unwavering support and belief in my abilities, pushing me to reach new heights.

Brian Ratliff, for your valuable contributions and insightful discussions that have shaped the book's concepts.

Your collective efforts and dedication have played an integral role in shaping and advancing this book. I am truly grateful for your unwavering support and collaboration throughout this journey. Thank you for being an essential part of this endeavor.

Introduction

In the fast-paced, often impersonal world of modern business, the art of corporate gifting is frequently overlooked or reduced to a mere afterthought. Yet, when approached strategically and executed thoughtfully, corporate gifting can be a powerful catalyst for building meaningful relationships, fostering unwavering loyalty, and driving substantial business growth. "The Corporate Gifting Playbook" is your comprehensive guide to unlocking this often untapped potential.

As the author, I embarked on a unique and immersive journey to explore the true impact of strategic corporate gifting. Over the course of an entire year, I created a line of premium scented candles aptly named "Lucky Penny Candles." These weren't just any candles; they were carefully crafted tokens of appreciation that I personally gifted to business owners across the United States and Canada. This hands-on experiment allowed me to observe and meticulously document the measurable results of thoughtful gifting strategies in real-world business scenarios.

You might be wondering, "Why should I care about corporate gifting?" The answer lies in the profound impact it can have on your business relationships and bottom line. From expressing heartfelt appreciation to valued employees as a talent retention tactic, to approaching prospective clients at local events, to showing genuine gratitude to loyal customers, strategic gifting can open doors, strengthen bonds, and create lasting impressions that translate into tangible business success.

This book is designed to benefit businesses of all sizes, from ambitious solopreneurs to established large corporations. Whether you're an entrepreneur looking to build stronger, more meaningful relationships, a marketing professional aiming to enhance brand recognition and customer loyalty, an HR specialist focusing on boosting employee morale and retention, or a sales professional seeking to close more deals and nurture client relationships, you'll find a wealth of valuable insights and actionable strategies within these pages.

Throughout "The Corporate Gifting Playbook," you'll discover:

- The psychology behind effective gift-giving in a business context, helping you understand the emotional and psychological impact of your gifting choices.
- How to choose the right gifts for different occasions and recipients, ensuring your gifts always hit the mark.
- The dos and don'ts of business gift-giving, helping you navigate potential pitfalls and cultural considerations.
- The crucial role of personalization in corporate gifting, and how to make each gift feel truly special.
- Strategies to leverage gifting for tangible business growth, turning your gifting budget into a powerful investment.
- Techniques for building and nurturing long-lasting relationships through thoughtful gifts.
- Winning strategies for your corporate gifting initiatives, from planning to execution.
- How to maximize the impact of gifting at promotional events, making your brand stand out in a crowd.

To bridge the gap between theory and practice, most chapters conclude with a real-world case study, providing concrete examples of the principles discussed. These case studies offer valuable insights into how various businesses, from startups to Fortune 500 companies, have successfully implemented strategic gifting to achieve their goals. You'll see firsthand how the strategies outlined in this book have been applied in diverse industries and situations, giving you the confidence to adapt these principles to your own unique business context.

For those eager to dive even deeper, full versions of these case studies are available on the book's companion website: www.GiftingPlaybook. com. But that's not all – the website also hosts a treasure trove of additional resources, including gifting strategy blueprints to help you prepare for your next corporate gifting event. These tools will allow you to immediately apply the knowledge gained from this book, turning insights into action.

"The Corporate Gifting Playbook" is more than just a guide—it's an invitation to transform your approach to business relationships. It challenges the notion that corporate gifting is a mere formality and reveals its potential as a strategic tool for business success. By the time you turn the last page, you'll be equipped with the knowledge, tools, and confidence to turn corporate gifting from a routine practice into a remarkable strategy that sets your business apart.

Let's embark on this journey together and unlock the true power of strategic corporate gifting. Your path to stronger relationships, enhanced loyalty, and accelerated business growth starts here.

DOM LEROUX
AUTHOR, "THE CORPORATE GIFTING PLAYBOOK"

CHAPTER 1

Showing Gratitude Through Giving

Giving Is a Part of Our Culture

There has always been widespread recognition and celebration of the social importance of giving.

Throughout history, many societies have recognized the importance of gift-giving as a means to express appreciation and devotion.

For instance, the Native American Potlatch ceremony was an elaborate gift-giving tradition that not only redistributed wealth within the community but also reinforced social bonds and status.

Similarly, in ancient Greece, the practice of 'Xenia' or guest-friendship involved the exchange of gifts to cement alliances and ensure the safety of travelers in foreign lands.

In the Pacific Northwest, Potlatch ceremonies were pivotal social events where leaders displayed their wealth and status by giving gifts. This act strengthened communal ties and established the host's status within the tribe. Similarly, during the medieval period, Byzantine aristocrats engaged in gift giving alongside emerging practices of commodity trading, using gifts to stimulate production and maintain social cohesion

Gift-giving has been and continues to be an integral aspect of social and economic interactions in several societies.

You do it. I do it. It's common practice among all of us.

To quote anthropologist Terry Y. Le Vine: "The act of giving and receiving presents is so prevalent that it is intrinsic to what it is to be human."

What individuals think of others, what they value, and what they like, as well as how they create and sustain connections, may all be gleaned through gift exchanges. Multiple facets of gift-giving and receiving are now being investigated by scholars. These include the decision-making processes of gift-givers and recipients, the recipients' uses for the presents, and the effects of gifts on the relationships between givers and receivers.

Le Vine was a visiting curator at UCLA's Fowler Museum of Cultural History, where they were putting up an exhibit comparing the significance of gift-giving across five different civilizations, including our own. "It's something everyone can identify to," said Le Vine, who has studied the practice of gift-giving for 15 years as a career.

Many presents are attractive in appearance (they do represent the taste of the giver, after all), so they are naturally suited to being shown off. Le Vine, however, argued that presents are more than just decorative items. She argued that in almost every culture, gift-giving and the celebrations around it are an integral part of the foundational process of establishing and maintaining social bonds. Gift giving acts as a social bond, strengthening communities. Even in countries where giving is prized above getting, it is common practice for benefactors to expect future favors in return for their generosity.

The potlatch is an example of a gift-giving celebration in which social standing is not based on material wealth but on the generosity with which gifts are given.

From the beginning of civilization, people understood the importance of giving to society. The potlatch is an ancient and elaborate ceremonial that has been practiced by some indigenous communities for thousands of years. Depending on the culture, a family's standing in the community may not have been determined by how much they owned but rather by how much they gave out. The more expensive and extravagant the potlatch, the more respect the host family receives.

Throughout time, people have recognized and appreciated the social importance of giving. Among many other examples, the potlatch is an elaborate event that honors exceptional acts of generosity. Families would host a potlatch to help out their neighbors and make sure everyone had enough food to eat. When we help others, we improve their mood and our own. By doing this, we also foster a feeling of belonging and solidarity.

There are many ways in which generosity may improve relationships with employees, clients and business partners. Giving to others has positive effects on both the receiver and the giver. We build a sense of belonging and mutual trust as well.

Relationships, both personal and professional, can benefit from the exchange of gifts. It's a great way to express your gratitude and appreciation. People's relationships can benefit from the trust and admiration fostered through presents.

The Giving Itself

Gift-giving can be done for various reasons, but it is always accompanied by some sort of sentiment. The act of presenting a gift brings happiness to both the giver and the recipient.

To understand the practice of gift-giving, it is essential to consider the evolution of the human species. Throughout millions of years, we have partnered and cooperated, which has shaped us into who we are today. By working together instead of isolating ourselves in separate communities, our species has a better chance of survival and prosperity. The feelings of joy and warmth associated with giving and receiving gifts are a result of our development as a species.

Over the years, psychologists, anthropologists, economists, and marketers have provided insights into the topic of gift-giving. They have discovered that gift-giving is a nuanced and crucial aspect of human interaction that helps shape and strengthen friendships and relationships. According to experts, the psychological benefits of giving a gift are often felt more by the giver than the recipient.

Tracy Ryan, an advertising professor at Virginia Commonwealth University, explains that when giving to another person, there is a sense of reciprocity and joy in knowing that you have taken care of someone. This pressure of reciprocity contributes to the joy experienced by the giver.

When we offer someone a gift, it is not out of necessity but because we genuinely want to. The act of making someone feel special is a rewarding experience for the giver, often inspiring further acts of generosity. Giving is a universal gesture of appreciation.

In this book, you'll learn about the science of gift-giving and how it may improve your relationships with your employees, clients and prospect clients.

The Power of Gift Giving

Have you ever just wondered *"What's the point of a gift?"*

It is a common practice to give presents to mark special events or show appreciation to others, whether the gifts are tangible or intangible. But why do we engage in this act of giving, often investing time and money without expecting anything in return?

Even when there is no immediate material gain from an act of kindness, there are still benefits to be obtained. Humans have evolved to participate in gift-giving for a specific reason: to facilitate social bonding and the formation of groups. This explains why gift-giving is pervasive across different cultural contexts and plays a significant role in nurturing interpersonal and professional relationships.

The Advantages of Gifting

Gift-giving is not just about the exchange of physical items; it's a way to strengthen bonds and show others they are valued. This tradition, rooted in ancient practices, continues to play a crucial role in society today. It promotes a sense of community and cooperation that has been essential for social development across various cultures.

Through gifts, we not only express our appreciation and build relationships, but we also encourage a cycle of generosity and reciprocity. This cultural and social mechanism helps maintain social ties and can even increase cooperation among individuals, improving group cohesion and stability.

Research supports the idea that acts of kindness, like gift-giving, can indeed boost one's energy levels, enjoyment, and even longevity. When individuals give gifts, it activates parts of the brain associated with pleasure and reward, providing a satisfaction similar to that experienced when receiving a gift. This brain activation is linked to the release of oxytocin and dopamine, which are associated with feelings of happiness and connection with others.

For instance, studies conducted by the National Institutes of Health using functional magnetic resonance imaging (fMRI) have shown that the brain's pleasure centers are activated not only when receiving money but also when deciding to donate money to a good cause [3]. This kind of voluntary giving increases the pleasure experienced, referred to as the "warm glow" effect.

Further research aligns with these findings, suggesting that such acts of generosity can also lead to better physical health and longevity [4]. Engaging in generous behaviors like gift-giving has been associated with lower blood pressure, reduced stress, and even a longer lifespan.

Overall, the psychological and physiological benefits of giving gifts underscore the powerful impact of this practice on both personal well-being and social bonds.

Empathy also plays a significant role in the art of giving presents. Finding the right gift requires understanding the wants, needs, and concerns of the recipient, showing that you care about them on a deeper level. Developing empathy through gift-giving can lead to closer relationships, improved emotional control, and a stronger sense of connection.

Acknowledging and appreciating someone's generosity without showering them with gifts can be as simple as expressing gratitude for their thoughtful gestures. A small note of thanks can pave the way for unexpected favors and strengthen the bond between individuals.

Gift-giving has a formative effect on our sense of self and can shape relationships and future outcomes. Accepting a gift creates a unique connection between the giver and the recipient, restoring harmony in the relationship. It brings joy to both parties, with the anticipation of the recipient's response adding excitement to the exchange.

Giving allows us to shift our perspective on wealth and move beyond materialistic values. It redirects our attention from ourselves to those in need and encourages us to contribute to social and political change. Acts of generosity alter our sense of identity, transforming us from mere observers to active contributors in making the world a better place.

Moreover, giving helps us find our unique place in the world, connecting with like-minded individuals and working together for greater impact. It allows us to navigate life transitions and ceremonies, symbolizing care, understanding, support, and appreciation for others.

While presents and gifts may overlap, a true gift is given selflessly because the giver wants the recipient to have it and knows they will appreciate it. It reflects genuine interest in the recipient's future and the desire to make a positive impact on their lives. Gift-giving should be valued and cherished in our culture, reminding us of its beauty and power.

Give something that is both out of the ordinary and memorable to guarantee that your giving will be treasured forever. Don't be scared to make a grand statement and think on a grand scale.

The Hidden Power of a Gift

In every kind of relationship, it is beneficial to consistently express to the people you care about how much you cherish them and value their presence and actions.

If you want to develop a strong and fulfilling relationship, giving gifts has always been an important part of the process.

While every relationship is unique in its own way, it's hard to dispute that gifts have a special way of solidifying the connection. Our discussion of relationships and bonding is not limited to just your significant other. It can be with anyone you regularly engage with, including family members, close friends, coworkers, and neighbors.

Sending blessings in the form of small gifts is a wonderful strategy for fostering closer ties between people. In a friendship or a relationship, it's important to always let the other person know how much they mean to you. No special occasion is required to shower someone with gifts. Giving them a token of your affection and appreciation on occasion will make them feel loved and appreciated.

The magic of gift-giving extends beyond just family members and intimate partners. In fact, you can harness this magical ability to build fulfilling and lasting bonds with literally anyone you come across. Regardless of who it may be and in whatever setting, giving a gift is one way to make them feel valued, appreciated, and at ease.

Whenever I make a sale, you and I exchange something of value with each other. If you pay me, I'll provide you with goods or a service. All parties involved have agreed to the terms of this exchange. To put it simply, we're both on an equal level. In fact, it's an even playing field.

The concept of gift-giving goes beyond the simple act of exchanging items; it involves deep emotional and social significance. But what makes a gift truly special? This question is not fully answered by simple explanations, as there are deeper elements involved, such as the magic of a ceremonial event like a potlatch, the emotional power of art, and the meaningfulness of a gift. These aspects help in forging stronger connections between people.

When someone gives you something for free, or provides you with much more than you expected, it creates a sort of imbalance that needs to be addressed. One way to understand this is by looking at traditional practices among Native Americans in the Pacific Northwest. During a potlatch, a chief would showcase his wealth and power by giving away all his possessions, which required others to recognize his status. This act of generosity wasn't just about giving away items but was also a demonstration of his ability to accumulate more, emphasizing his leadership and influence.

However, if this interpretation doesn't quite fit, consider the example of an artist. When an artist displays artwork in a gallery or releases a song, they aren't directly compensated by those who view or listen to their work. Instead, their offering gains value through public recognition and appreciation. If the art is compelling, it inspires viewers or listeners to become advocates of the artist's work, spreading their admiration to others.

There are also times when we reciprocate a gift not with another item, but by showing loyalty or preference to the giver or their brand. Receiving a gift can make us feel valued and appreciated, strengthening our connection with the giver.

The dynamics of gift-giving can be problematic in scenarios like international aid. Often, the generosity of wealthy donors can be seen as controlling, which might lead to resentment rather than gratitude. This kind of giving can feel less like genuine generosity and more like an exercise of power.

Nothing compares to the impact of a well-executed gift. When we accept gifts with gratitude, our lives undergo a transformation. The discord prompts action, which compels us to seek a new balance and ultimately forges a bond between us.

The most important aspect is that the recipient genuinely appreciates the gift. Simply sending something to someone without thought isn't a gift; it's advertising. Gifts should be offered sincerely, without any expectation of reciprocation. Being an artist or a member of a community (such as willingly paying taxes for a school you will never again send your adult children to) requires a certain set of skills because the act of giving motivates you to do even better work.

The act of gifting itself has a positive emotional effect. Giving is a celebration of kindness. To give a gift properly means to prioritize the recipient's interests over our own and to spend time considering a suitable present.

Giving thoughtful gifts requires us to move beyond mere talk about the values we believe in and instead embody those values through generous actions.

There are positive emotions experienced by the giver as well as positive outcomes for the recipient when they receive a gift.

It is believed that "if it is friend to friend, people will remain considerate." In a romantic relationship, people also try to appeal to each other's emotions. If we want to connect with someone, gift-giving speaks to that desire.

Numerous studies have shown that giving presents can help the giver feel better about themselves.

When individuals are giving from abroad, it becomes even more significant, according to researchers. "These days, buying and sending a gift couldn't be easier with the help of the Internet. It serves as a good substitute for physically being present. Finding the perfect gift brings them joy and contentment."

Positive psychology suggests that if you act positively, you will attract positivity. Although altruism is rarely motivated by the expectation of personal gain, there is a saying that goes, "If I perform a kind act, something good will come to me."

The impact of a thoughtful gift cannot be overstated. If you're wondering "How so?" you're not alone. Let's explore the benefits of giving, and you will soon realize the power of generosity.

Giving to others has numerous evident effects, the most notable of which is the induction of warm and positive sentiments in the recipient.

Here are a few examples:

- Happiness at being pleasantly surprised.
- Feelings of delight upon receiving a gift.
- Feeling appreciated because someone took the time to think of you.
- Having the comforting realization that you have friends and family all across the globe.

Giving can evoke all those wonderful emotions and more. However, did you realize that the right gift can have a significant impact on the lives of the people you care about? It may sound like a big claim, but it is supported by evidence.

We all have aspirations for how we want our lives to unfold in the long run. For some, that means being more physically active; for others, it involves expanding their horizons through travel or education, and for some, it means starting their own successful business. The challenge lies in forming new habits and breaking old ones. But how exactly can someone's ambitions be aided by receiving a gift?

A well-considered gift that aligns with the aspirations of the individuals you care about will not only encourage them to keep working toward their goals but also serve as a constant reminder of your unwavering support. Giving them something that reflects their aspirations will convey how much you believe in what they are trying to accomplish. The simple act of knowing you care will inspire renewed enthusiasm in the hearts of your loved ones for whatever they are pursuing. As you can see, the impact of a thoughtful gift can be tremendous.

A gift comes with the implicit understanding that it may be reciprocated in some way, but the thought and effort put into a present hold more value than its monetary worth. The practicality of a gift is less important than the meaning it carries for the recipient. Research even suggests that the recipient will strive to replicate the emotional impact of the gift. Giving back to the community is essential, and it's no wonder the saying "you get out of life what you put in" resonates across cultures.

So, what does this imply for you? Giving someone a thoughtful gift not only brings all the benefits we've described, but the giver can also anticipate receiving benefits in return. This magical process creates a positive feedback loop of supportive sentiments and energy, resulting in healthy and enduring relationships.

How does it all come together? A small gesture of affection can have far-reaching effects on both you and those you care about, initiating a beautiful chain reaction of joy. Not only does it make you feel good, but it also demonstrates that the recipient holds a special place in your thoughts. In today's busy world, where it's easy to get caught up in work, financial concerns, and obligations, there's something truly wonderful about this act.

To summarize, these are the reasons why gift-giving is crucial. Sending unexpected gifts to the people you care about is an excellent way to deepen your connections with them and bring a radiant smile to their faces. Not only does it spread and cultivate happiness, but it also makes you unforgettable and strengthens your relationships.

A Real-World Example of Employee Appreciation Through Strategic Gifting: Hawaii's Special Education Staff

In the realm of corporate gifting, the focus often falls on clients and customers. However, this case study demonstrates the powerful impact of applying gifting strategies to show appreciation for employees, particularly in challenging and often overlooked professions like special education.

On September 23, 2022, a unique gifting campaign was initiated to show appreciation for the Special Education staff of the Hawaii Department of Education. This initiative, spearheaded by the founder of Lucky Penny Candles in Venice, Florida, showcased how strategic corporate gifting can be effectively applied in the public sector, particularly in education.

The campaign was born from a personal connection to education and insider insight. As a former college instructor, the initiative's creator felt a deep understanding of the challenges faced by educators, especially in light of the COVID-19 pandemic. This understanding was further enhanced by a conversation with Amber Weber, a Certified Occupational Therapy Assistant in the Leeward District, who provided valuable perspective on the staff's efforts.

The gifting strategy was carefully crafted to maximize its impact. Rather than a broad, generalized approach, the campaign targeted a specific group - the special education staff - who often work behind the scenes and may feel underappreciated. This targeted approach made the gesture particularly meaningful.

The choice of gift was equally thoughtful. Natural Lucky Penny candles were selected as a token of appreciation. These candles, being both practical and long-lasting, served as a constant reminder of the appreciation shown. The choice of a natural product also aligned well with the nurturing nature of education work.

The execution of the campaign was streamlined and direct. Jody Agpalsa, District Education Specialist of the Pearl City/Waipahu complex, was contacted directly to facilitate the distribution of the gifts. This direct approach ensured that the gifts reached their intended recipients efficiently.

While specific feedback wasn't received, the campaign likely resulted in several positive outcomes. The unexpected gesture of appreciation likely boosted staff morale, particularly valuable in the challenging post-COVID period. The initiative also fostered positive relations between a private business and public education, demonstrating the power of cross-sector goodwill.

To amplify the impact of the gifting campaign, a press release was issued on the day of the initiative. This public acknowledgment served multiple purposes. It brought attention to the often-underappreciated work of special education staff, raised awareness about the extraordinary efforts of education staff during the pandemic, and provided public recognition that extended beyond the gift itself.

This case study highlights several key principles for effective employee appreciation through corporate gifting:

1. Leverage personal connections to make gifting more meaningful and authentic.
2. Target overlooked groups to make the gesture particularly impactful.
3. Time your gifting initiatives strategically to acknowledge specific challenges or periods of extra effort.
4. Seek insider input to inform your gifting strategy.
5. Use a direct approach for smooth execution of your gifting initiative.
6. Amplify your impact through public recognition.
7. Consider cross-sector initiatives to create broader goodwill and positive PR.
8. Choose gifts that reflect the values of both the giver and the recipients.

By thoughtfully implementing these strategies, businesses can use corporate gifting as a powerful tool for employee appreciation. This approach not only boosts morale but also fosters a positive corporate culture, enhances public relations, and demonstrates a company's commitment to its employees and the broader community. In an era where employee satisfaction and public perception are increasingly crucial, such initiatives can play a vital role in a company's overall success strategy.

CHAPTER 2

Becoming a Kindness Centric Company

One of the challenges of demonstrating compassion in the workplace is that it is sometimes stereotypically associated with femininity. In many work environments, men may be more socially accepted when they are direct and assertive, while women who take a more indirect approach can be perceived as ineffective or weak.

However, leading with kindness, whether through a kind remark or a considerate gesture, is undeniably more pleasant than issuing orders or sending curt emails. Demonstrating compassion towards your colleagues and business partners not only improves relationships but can also contribute to increased profitability.

Look Beyond the Title When Hiring

When hiring, it's important to look beyond job titles and consider the qualities that truly matter. Sincerity and honesty are often well-received attributes. During interviews, pay attention to how candidates interact with others, the level of detail they provide about their professional and personal experiences, and the tone and content of their thank-you notes. Employees who consistently demonstrate warmth, sincerity, and joy tend to have longer tenures with a company.

It's worth noting that kindness is not something that can be taught to others. People either possess it or they don't. This is a lesson I've learned through experience.

Keep a Grateful Attitude No Matter What

While it's easy to express gratitude and kindness when things are going well at work, it requires more effort to do so in the face of adversity. Even if you can't immediately see the benefits of a challenging situation, it's important to trust that it will have a positive impact in the future. Instead of reacting with anger or frustration, focus on the lessons to be learned and keep moving forward. Remember that a brighter morning is often just around the corner.

Let go of the need to control everything. In the past, I used to meticulously plan for every possible outcome and stress over various scenarios. However, I've come to realize that I can only control a limited portion of my day. What I can control are my own responses and reactions. Embracing kindness and consideration brings about a sense of fulfillment and eliminates regret. Looking at myself in the mirror at night, I feel proud rather than embarrassed.

Prioritizing compassion over profit is not only a wise business decision but also contributes to a better sleep at night. Optimism, compassion, and a cheerful attitude are highly contagious. Through my experiences, I've learned that everyone is going through their own struggles, and showing even a little compassion can go a long way in alleviating their suffering. Ask yourself, do you want to be remembered for putting someone in their place or for making someone happy?

Kindness is one of my core principles, and it permeates every aspect of my life and work. Recognizing it as one of my strengths, I have made a conscious decision to incorporate generosity into my company's model. It is entirely possible to be compassionate, powerful, passionate, and focused. You can have clear goals for your company's strategy while still treating others with kindness. Being genuine and honest in your interactions with others does not mean you have to sacrifice consideration.

Integrating kindness into your business strategy starts with yourself. Your own efforts are the first step. In many of my interactions, I emphasize the importance of kindness. It probably comes as no surprise to hear me say that you must be the first to demonstrate compassion. As the sole employee of your company, it can be easy to become overwhelmed and burned out. I recall an incident from a networking event some time ago. After the presentation, we engaged in open discussion, and someone asked me when was the last time I had taken a vacation. I was taken aback because I couldn't remember. Interestingly, many others in the audience shared the same experience. Take a moment to reflect on that question.

How Does Compassion Manifest Itself in Your Company?

Considering kindness as a business tactic is worth exploring. Word-of-mouth recommendations are invaluable for companies aiming to expand their customer base. Engaging in acts of giving and helping others is crucial for this strategy. Take a moment to think about a business that pleasantly surprised you with acts of kindness or generosity. What result did you expect? It's understandable why you felt compelled to share your experience with others. Perhaps it solidified your loyalty to that business.

Placing a greater emphasis on kindness as a principle and business practice yields a positive return on investment. By connecting with clients on an emotional level and creating warm, positive memories of previous interactions, you set yourself apart from the competition. If your kindness is something they haven't encountered elsewhere, it's natural for them to choose you.

While some may consider showing empathy and compassion in the workplace foolish, I disagree. When a culture of kindness and compassion is fostered, everyone benefits. The best work is often accomplished in an environment of mutual respect and appreciation. It's not an impossible dream.

When I join a new company, one of my initial priorities is to reintroduce a culture of love and compassion. In my experience, this has the potential to completely transform an organization. By cultivating a culture of kindness and compassion, you'll have happier, more dedicated employees who strive to do their best. Moreover, you'll experience less stress.

Kindness alone is not enough; gratitude must also be shown. Expressing thanks and appreciation for someone's efforts has a positive impact on them. The work atmosphere quickly improves, making it a place where people genuinely want to be.

Include it in your values and conduct.

Let's discuss the significance of a "culture of kindness" within your company. It should go beyond mere empty phrases. What behaviors do you expect from your staff members? And how would kindness and compassion specifically benefit your business?

Leaders are often advised to "be the change they want to see." If you aim to foster a culture of compassion, it must start with you. Put compassion into practice in every aspect of your work, making it the norm within your organization. Simple acts like offering a kind greeting, making eye contact, and genuinely caring about others can make a significant difference. It's not just about giving advice; it's about being willing to follow that advice yourself.

Always give others the benefit of the doubt, even if they've made a mistake or caused a problem. We all have our limitations as humans. Acting kindly and compassionately involves considering the other person's perspective and working together to find solutions. Avoid rushing to judgment or assuming the worst.

These actions greatly contribute to creating a society where compassion is valued. By basing your interactions with your staff on compassion and empathy, you will foster trust, respect, and loyalty. Check in with your employees to see how they are doing, offer support if they seem to be struggling, and express gratitude for their efforts.

Being considerate means treating others with respect, which includes creating an environment where they feel safe to share their thoughts and feelings without fear of retaliation. To cultivate a caring culture, businesses need to consider the emotional needs of their employees and create an atmosphere that supports their well-being.

Set an example of compassion within your group. Engaging in volunteer activities as a team can foster camaraderie and spread generosity. Can your group participate in sponsored events, raise funds for a good cause, or collect food for a local food bank? Take actions that prioritize service to others and exemplify the values you want to see at the forefront of your company.

What steps will you take to make kindness a hallmark of your company's culture?

A Look at the Upsides of Being Generous

There are several advantages to cultivating kindness in our interactions. First and foremost, being kind to our coworkers has significant benefits. Gallup's annual polls consistently show that expressing appreciation to staff members reduces burnout, decreases absenteeism, and boosts overall morale. Numerous studies have demonstrated the positive effects of receiving compliments, acknowledgment, and praise on individuals' sense of fulfillment, self-esteem, and self-evaluation. Compliments reinforce our positive self-opinions, leading to increased happiness and well-being.

Secondly, practicing generosity brings greater satisfaction to our own lives. Giving to others, whether through monetary means or by offering our time, has been linked to increased happiness and a sense of purpose. Acts of kindness hold more value as they extend beyond ourselves, positively influencing how others perceive us and shaping our own self-perception. Acts of kindness provide evidence of our own goodness, boosting our confidence and long-term contentment, especially in remote work situations where finding reasons to smile can be challenging.

Thirdly, recent research suggests that giving a compliment can bring as much, if not more, joy than receiving one. In a study where individuals shared their experiences and then offered sincere compliments to their partners, it was found that making someone else happy was more rewarding than receiving a compliment. The happiness derived from acts of kindness is often underestimated.

The question arises: why does complimenting others bring us such happiness? The answer lies in the significance of social connections, which have been greatly impacted by the pandemic. Delivering compliments and small gifts that focus the recipient's attention on the giver strengthens the bond between individuals. While it's wonderful to receive compliments, giving genuine compliments requires us to consider how they will make the other person feel. It involves putting ourselves in their shoes and truly connecting with them. Compliments and acts of kindness have the power to strengthen relationships, foster optimism in interactions, and uplift our own spirits.

However, many people feel uncomfortable giving compliments. Why is that? Recent studies by Erica Boothby and Vanesa Bohn indicate that the mere thought of approaching someone and complimenting them can trigger social anxiety and discomfort. This common assumption leads us to believe that compliments would make people feel uneasy and annoyed, when in reality, the opposite is often true.

The shift to remote work has added additional challenges to expressing gratitude, generosity, and appreciation towards others. In pre-pandemic times, businesses had official programs to recognize and appreciate their employees, and spontaneous expressions of gratitude would occur during chance encounters. However, in the era of Zoom meetings and rigid schedules, there is often limited opportunity for side conversations or the exchange of compliments.

Establishing a culture that promotes compassion and acts of kindness is highly beneficial for businesses. When compassion becomes a regular part of the workplace, it can have a ripple effect.

Research supports the numerous benefits of kindness in the workplace. For instance, a study highlighted by HRMorning reveals that acts of kindness can lead to increased productivity, higher satisfaction, and greater well-being among employees. This is because kindness promotes a positive work environment, which can lower stress levels and enhance overall employee health, leading to fewer sick days and more engagement at work [1].

Furthermore, the Stanford Graduate School of Business discusses how kindness fosters a culture of generosity and compassion within organizations. When leaders demonstrate kindness, it sets a tone that encourages others to replicate these behaviors, creating a cycle of positivity that benefits both individuals and the organization as a whole. This type of environment not only improves employee retention but also contributes to achieving corporate goals by building a supportive and collaborative workplace [2].

Bringing Happiness to the Office

To what extent can top executives promote compassion in the office? They can start by leading by example and practicing what they preach. People naturally pay attention to the actions of those in positions of authority, so leaders can set the tone for their teams by openly praising and complimenting their work.

Secondly, supervisors can incorporate a "kindness round" during Zoom meetings, where employees are given the opportunity to freely compliment each other on their efforts. It doesn't require much time, just a few minutes each week. However, in projects that take months to complete and are primarily conducted through virtual platforms, even those few minutes can significantly boost morale and foster social interaction.

Lastly, consider offering small, one-time incentives. Companies like Google have implemented "peer bonus" systems, where employees are encouraged to reward exceptional performance by granting modest monetary rewards from a company-wide pool. People appreciate acts of kindness regardless of their size, so even small gestures can make a difference. Sending a gift card or a small present via mail may suffice. The psychological benefits of acts of kindness can be triggered by simple recognition, and they don't have to be costly or time-consuming to implement.

Acts of compassion can help counteract the negative impacts of our increasingly digital social lives. It is a crucial leadership trait that has the potential to spread throughout an organization, ultimately transforming the ethos of its employees.

Today's corporate world seems to have lost its appreciation for generosity. Increasingly, individuals believe that a leader must project an intimidating persona to be effective. Additionally, showing compassion is often misconstrued as a sign of weakness. This situation is tragic for two reasons:

Firstly, a pleasant work environment is crucial for fostering efficiency among staff members. When employees feel comfortable and supported, they are more likely to perform their best and contribute positively to the organization.

Secondly, a manager's kindness, when utilized correctly, can have a significant impact. Research in the field of primatology, led by experts like Frans de Waal, has demonstrated that humans, like other members of the primate family, have a natural inclination to care for one another. Additionally, psychologists have highlighted the crucial role of the first two years of a person's life in the development of empathy.

Considering the importance of empathy for the continued improvement of our species, it begs the question why we don't prioritize it more in the workplace, where we spend an average of 10 hours each day. On weekdays, we devote around two-thirds of our waking hours, or 63% of our time, to activities other than sleeping (assuming an average of 8 hours of sleep per day). It is disheartening that our lives are mostly spent in a culture that does not value compassion and generosity.

A well-known example, The Roseto Effect highlights how close-knit community relationships can significantly impact physical health, particularly heart health. This phenomenon was first observed in the 1960s in Roseto, Pennsylvania, a town with a predominantly Italian-American population. Researchers discovered that despite a diet rich in fats, the community had a remarkably low rate of heart disease compared to the national average. They attributed this to the strong social bonds and the supportive environment prevalent in the town.

The key factor believed to contribute to the residents' good health was the high level of social cohesion and support among community members. This social structure provided emotional and psychological comfort, reducing stress and, consequently, reducing the risk of heart disease. Over time, as the community became more assimilated into the broader American culture, losing some of its tight-knit social structure, the incidence of heart disease rose to levels more typical of other American towns.

It is not difficult to imagine the negative consequences of spending the majority of one's waking hours in a hostile workplace. Stressed, demotivated, and dissatisfied employees are likely to activate their biological evolutionary defense mechanism, leading to high staff turnover, which is detrimental to any organization, and a drastic decline in productivity.

Recognizing the importance of kindness and compassion in the workplace is crucial for creating a supportive and thriving environment where employees can thrive, resulting in improved well-being, engagement, and overall organizational success.

Being kind and compassionate can indeed help individuals advance in their careers. However, it is puzzling why many companies continue to employ and reward managers who lack compassion in the workplace, despite data indicating the benefits of empathy and sincerity for everyone involved. The concern among leaders is that showing compassion may diminish their power, reputation, and ability to achieve results. However, this belief is entirely unfounded.

The issue lies in the fact that demonstrating sympathy and goodwill in the workplace can be done effectively or inappropriately. Unfortunately, inexperienced leaders often default to the "wrong way," resulting in toxic, politicized, and ultimately non-meritocratic work environments. The good news is that there is a "right way" to demonstrate empathy, but it requires practice and maturity to get there.

Let's first examine the common incorrect strategy. It occurs when a supervisor avoids providing constructive criticism to an employee for their poor performance. This is done under the guise of caring for the employee's well-being and to conform to political correctness. However, the feedback is so vague and pleasant-sounding that the employee may not even realize they are being criticized. As a result, their output remains subpar, creating tension, particularly among high-performing employees who cannot thrive in a system that lacks merit-based evaluations.

Therefore, empathy is crucial in the workplace. The question then becomes: How do we cultivate it?

As a first step, we need to seek out candidates who possess empathetic qualities. Equally important is finding managers who can maintain a pleasant and productive working relationship. I believe this is the secret to fostering a thriving workplace culture. While it is true that a positive work culture develops organically over time, we must remember that it all starts with management and leadership. Managers set the standard for how employees should be treated and managed through their own actions and words. By prioritizing empathy, leaders can create an environment where compassion is valued, leading to happier employees, improved performance, and a stronger organization as a whole.

When you challenge your team and encourage them to do the same, it creates an environment where members feel safe to share their opinions. This demonstrates to your staff that you value honesty and are willing to admit when you are wrong, taking responsibility for any mistakes made by you or the organization. By caring about your team as individuals and professionals with their own goals, you reassure them that their best interests are a priority.

I have personally experienced some of the most rewarding professional partnerships by taking an interest in others and pushing them beyond their comfort zones. This is more of an art form than a scientific endeavor and cannot be forced. However, it is a skill that can be taught and developed.

Being a compassionate leader requires courage, especially in companies that prioritize profit above all else. It takes bravery, honesty, and resilience, but the benefits are worth it. Employees who are treated with kindness have a stronger sense of belonging in the workplace, which increases their motivation, productivity, and creativity.

When leaders are genuine and kind to their teams, trust naturally increases, leading to improved collaboration, morale, and productivity. The positive effects of leadership through kindness extend beyond productivity. Kindness is contagious, and it will influence your behavior not only at work but also in other areas of your life, such as at home and in the community.

It is important to express your true feelings, as your staff can quickly discern whether you are being sincere. Taking the time to write a handwritten letter of appreciation to an employee who has gone above and beyond on a project can have a significant impact. Make an effort to spend time with your staff outside of work-related activities. Attend important life events such as funerals or engage in conversations about upcoming milestones like the birth of a child, a move, or a sporting competition. These actions demonstrate genuine care and build stronger connections with your team members.

Great things can happen when you dedicate even a few minutes every day to actively building relationships with your team. Additionally, creating a pleasant and inviting atmosphere with delightful and fragrant candles can work wonders.

One effective method to connect with your team on a deeper level is to discuss what motivates each individual member. You can start by sharing your top three values, such as honesty, integrity, and collaboration, and then ask them about their own values. Understanding and sharing each other's priorities can foster stronger connections within the team. When employees' core values align with those of the company, it leads to higher levels of job satisfaction and productivity. Openly discussing shared ideals can help everyone stay accountable.

Treating staff members well results in higher levels of appreciation and social connection, which in turn boosts productivity and cooperation. It's important to acknowledge their efforts and provide constructive criticism when needed. Workers value any form of recognition for their work, not just monetary compensation, as numerous studies have shown. One of the best ways to show your appreciation is to publicly recognize their achievements during team meetings or through an email to the entire team.

Being able to communicate openly and honestly is crucial in a team setting. When team members feel safe sharing their thoughts and opinions with their superiors, they are more likely to receive criticism positively. A manager who genuinely cares about an employee's success and provides helpful feedback is offering one of the best gifts they can give.

Being a kind person requires thought, effort, and persistence. It's important to periodically check in with yourself to assess your intellectual, emotional, and physical well-being. This self-awareness will help you stay focused. If you notice yourself becoming tense, taking three or four deep breaths with a full exhale can help relax your nervous system before heading into a meeting or engaging in a discussion. Other successful tactics include taking breaks from work, going outdoors for a breath of fresh air, and incorporating regular meditation into your routine.

Inspiring leadership has its merits, but when combined with compassion, it becomes extraordinary. Leadership based on kindness has a positive impact on the lives of individuals, communities, and the world as a whole. As poet Mary Oliver eloquently stated, there is something in the human spirit that relies on the presence of kindness. We instinctively anticipate it, and when we experience it, we are able to trust and open ourselves up to others.

CHAPTER 3

Choosing the Right Gifts

Understanding the Essence of Corporate Gifts

Gift-giving holds significance in many corporate cultures. The under-lying motivation for giving gifts remains the same, whether you aim to express gratitude to long-standing clients, reinforce your firm's presence, or recognize outstanding employees.

Corporate gifts are seen as a vital tool for enhancing both existing and new business endeavors. They play a crucial role in maintaining and strengthening current relationships. Attracting new clients and expanding market share through effective marketing is essential for the success of any business. By acknowledging both current employees and new customers, the right type of corporate gifts can help reach the target market, generate fresh referrals, and increase leads.

Corporate Gifts: What Exactly Are They?

The significance of regularly expressing gratitude to employees and customers has increased in recent years. Low employee morale or customer dissatisfaction can harm a company's reputation, making it challenging to attract new customers in the future.

As a result, businesses are striving to develop strategies that demonstrate appreciation and nurture the relationships that form the foundation of their operations. Corporate gifting, a time-tested approach, is naturally employed to achieve this goal.

Whether it's a tangible item like branded merchandise, delicious food, or unique clothing, or a digital gift such as an eGift card or tickets to a fun event, corporate giving serves as a wonderful way to show appreciation to employees, clients, and potential customers. Receiving a gift has a profound impact as it strengthens the recipient's connection to the giver and can foster positive associations between the recipient and the giver's business. Companies and marketers have long relied on the power of gifts to solidify relationships with both existing and new consumers while expressing gratitude for their support. When integrated into a broader marketing or employee retention strategy, gifting can yield significant ROI and enhance overall satisfaction.

Corporate gifts can be categorized into two broad categories: those given to customers and those given to staff. Both types of business gift giving can offer significant benefits to your company.

When it comes to employee morale and reducing turnover rates, corporate gift packets are just one of the many strategies you can employ. Offering corporate gift packs is an effective way to strengthen relationships with both current and prospective customers, while also distinguishing your company from competitors.

Why Give Corporate Gifts?

Receiving a meaningful gift is indeed an effective way to demonstrate appreciation to someone.

Both customers and employees who do not feel appreciated pose significant risks to any business. Customers who feel undervalued are more likely to seek alternatives and take their business elsewhere. Studies suggest that as many as seven out of ten customers may leave a company due to poor service or a perceived lack of appreciation.

Likewise, employees who feel unappreciated are prone to becoming demotivated and less productive. In the worst-case scenario, they may actively seek employment elsewhere, where they believe their contributions will be recognized and valued.

While it is invaluable for managers and executives to personally express gratitude, thoughtful corporate gifts or gift packs can also play a significant role in conveying appreciation to employees. Something as simple as a notepad with a handwritten message or a set of branded headphones can go a long way in making the recipient feel valued.

Regularly giving corporate gifts to recognize exceptional performance, show appreciation, and acknowledge employees who go above and beyond can have a positive impact on workplace morale. Creating a more positive and upbeat work environment can increase employee satisfaction and motivation, leading to improved performance and a greater sense of anticipation when coming to work. This benefits everyone involved.

In terms of customer relationships, the quality of connection plays a crucial role in a customer's decision to choose your company over competitors. Merely contacting customers on billing days may not build a strong connection. However, by actively working on building and strengthening the relationship, including regular communication and sending corporate gifts throughout the year, you can create happier clients. This enhanced connection increases the likelihood of maintaining a long-term business relationship.

It's worth noting that a study found that recipients of promotional gifts have a 66% recall rate for the brands associated with those gifts [5]. This highlights the effectiveness of corporate gifts in brand recognition and recall.

Considering the potential for generating goodwill, corporate gifts can be highly valuable for a company in both the present and the future.

They have a positive impact on the three key groups that matter most to a business: employees, clients, and potential customers.

All of Your Employees

It's evident that gift-giving to staff can have a positive impact on morale, happiness, and overall efficiency in the workplace. This, in turn, can help reduce staff turnover and contribute to building a stable and long-term workforce.

Moreover, providing presents to employees presents an excellent opportunity to communicate the brand's history and instill the values and ideals that you want them to embrace. Introducing gift-giving at important moments during the employment cycle can significantly boost job satisfaction. For example, during the onboarding process, presenting new employees with something as simple as a welcome kit that includes essentials like a company mug or notebook can make them feel welcome and valued. This initial gesture helps set a positive tone and shows that the company cares about its employees from day one.

Additionally, recognizing employees' achievements and milestones with gifts can reinforce their sense of belonging and appreciation. For example, giving a small bonus or a gift card for a local restaurant after the successful completion of a project not only acknowledges the hard work but also encourages a culture of recognition and reward. Celebrating personal milestones like birthdays with a token of appreciation, such as a small gift or an extra day off, can further enhance job satisfaction and employee loyalty.

These thoughtful acts of giving at critical moments help create a supportive work environment where employees feel recognized and valued, which is crucial for maintaining high levels of job satisfaction. This approach not only helps in retaining talent but also in attracting new employees who are looking for a positive and rewarding workplace.

It is important to emphasize the significance of both quality and consistency in corporate gift-giving. Occasional gestures every decade or so may not yield significant results, especially if the gift does not match the importance of the occasion. It is more effective to regularly reward achievements and hard work with presents that hold meaning for the recipients.

Patrons and Purchasers

Research has shown that offering corporate gifts to clients and customers can have a similar positive effect as giving gifts to employees. It not only strengthens your relationship with them but also gives you a competitive edge in your industry, which is an added advantage.

Having unique corporate swag can set your business apart from the competition and position you as a market leader. By offering thoughtful gifts, you stay top of mind with your customers and evoke positive emotions, which directly translates into increased sales, revenue, and brand awareness.

One of the greatest benefits of corporate gifting is the encouragement to take action that these presents provide. By demonstrating your care and appreciation for your clients, you motivate them to reciprocate with further praise, recommendations, and sales.

Potential Customers

Lastly, it's important to consider the needs of your potential customers as well. By offering corporate gifts, you have the potential to generate more leads and achieve a higher conversion rate, which is beneficial for your business. Moreover, these gifts can increase brand favorability, resulting in a more positive impression of your brand among your target consumers.

What Makes a Gift Meaningful?

This is something that every one of us can relate to. When shopping for a loved one, we often strive to find a meaningful gift that will make a lasting impression.

However, it can be challenging to determine what exactly constitutes a meaningful gift. To begin, let's identify what doesn't make a meaningful gift. Generic items like pens and notepads, for example, may be practical but lack the personal touch and special message that make a gift truly meaningful.

Here are two examples of situations where the gift given was not meaningful:

1. Employee Appreciation Day

A company decides to give every worker the same coffee mug printed with the company's logo for Employee Appreciation Day. The gift, meant to celebrate the employees' hard work, ends up feeling impersonal because it shows no effort to recognize individual contributions or interests. It's just a generic item that doesn't reflect the special occasion or the value of the employees.

2. Trade Show

At a trade show, a company hands out pens with their logo to every client who visits their booth. One client, expecting something more thoughtful or unique, feels annoyed rather than valued. The pen is practical but does nothing to make the client feel specially recognized or excited about the company's services, leading to a missed opportunity to make a positive impression.

It's crucial to recognize the negative impact that a generic gift can have. Presenting something ordinary and unremarkable runs the risk of making the recipient feel undervalued, as if the gift was chosen out of obligation rather than genuine thoughtfulness. This is certainly not the impression you want to convey.

On the other hand, think about the joy and warmth you feel when someone presents you with a meaningful and special gift. It's a delightful sensation to know that someone invested their time and effort, going above and beyond to find something they believed would truly impress you. That's the kind of impact you should strive for when choosing a gift.

Take a moment to consider the impact of a truly appreciated gift. Such gifts are not only cherished in the present moment but hold significance throughout the recipient's lifetime. They serve as a constant reminder of the value you place on their presence in your life and the love and support they have provided. Meaningful gifts transcend mere material possessions; they symbolize something much deeper.

Fortunately, we are here to guide you through the process of choosing a meaningful gift. We will cover what to do, what to avoid, and provide you with questions to consider. Here are some key points to focus on:

Gratitude

It is common to overlook the importance of life and the people around us when we are young. As we grow older, we come to realize the preciousness and brevity of life. This realization drives us to express our gratitude to those who are closest to us, acknowledging how fortunate we are to have them in our lives.

However, expressing gratitude is not always effortless. It requires effort and thoughtfulness to effectively convey our feelings and reach our intended audience.

Love

Yes, even in the corporate world, love is a powerful force that transcends boundaries. Expressing the depth of love can be challenging because it is a universal emotion that holds immense power. While poems, music, letters, and verbal declarations of love can all help, it is often the small gestures that truly make love felt - a smile, a gentle touch, or a comforting presence.

The act of giving a gift is no exception. If you want to express your affection and create a lasting memory for someone, consider giving them a meaningful gift such as a framed painting or a wallet-sized card. With a touch of creativity, you can even extend this gesture into the corporate realm.

Faith

Faith serves as a source of strength and resilience in both good times and bad. It reminds us to be grateful for our blessings during moments of happiness and empowers us to face challenges with courage. Faith is a precious gift that can be shared with those we care about.

Now, let's talk about bringing your plans for corporate gifts into reality. It can be tempting to simply give any expensive item as a gift, but there is much more to corporate gifts than meets the eye. Before making significant purchases, consider the following questions to ensure that you meet the needs and preferences of your target audience.

Is the Present Appropriate for the Occasion and Recipient?

While a gift bag filled with treats may be well-received by a new hire, it might not generate the same level of enthusiasm from a long-term employee who has been with the company for 10 years. To avoid any potential issues, it's important to do your research. The key to achieving desired results lies in selecting a gift that is suitable for both the recipient and the occasion, and this requires some thoughtful consideration.

In this context, the relationship with the recipient and the specific occasion are the two most critical factors to consider. Especially when dealing with someone who has been with your company for a decade or more, it is acceptable to aim for an emotional connection through the gift. The same principle applies to Christmas workplace parties, where the gifts should align with the spirit of the season.

Is It Close Enough to Home?

While it may be appropriate to give identical gifts to everyone during business functions, if your goal is to truly impress someone, it's important to consider what would be most meaningful and appreciated by them as an individual.

The value of a gift is not solely determined by its price tag. Often, the most meaningful gestures come from simple and thoughtful presents. However, it's worth noting that some individuals may be more interested in experiences rather than material items. Taking the time to learn about their passions and pursuits can provide valuable insight into what would make a meaningful gift for them.

Can We Expect Strong Name Recognition?

You want the recipients of your gifts to remember and cherish them, but it's common for gifts to get lost or overlooked amidst the influx of items received during holidays and special occasions. To prevent this from happening, it's important to include a heartfelt letter and message along with your gift. This personal touch can make a significant difference in ensuring that your gift stands out and is appreciated.

To further enhance the remembrance of your presents, consider marking them with your company's name and/or a personal message. This not only reinforces your brand identity but also adds a special touch that can leave a lasting impression on the recipient. By incorporating these elements, you increase the chances of your gifts being remembered long after they have been opened.

Where Do You Stand on the Price/Value?

It's important to consider your financial situation when planning corporate gifting. It would defeat the purpose if the gifts provided were of poor quality. However, it's equally important to avoid overspending, as this could strain your company's finances and hinder its ability to meet other obligations.

Ideally, you would have budgeted for corporate gifts well in advance of making your purchases. Set aside a designated amount for future gift purchases and consider whether the occasion calls for a more extravagant gift. Also, take into account whether the recipient deserves a more luxurious option based on their contribution or significance to your business.

By striking a balance between quality and financial prudence, you can ensure that your corporate gifts are thoughtful and meaningful without jeopardizing your company's financial stability.

Does It Accurately Reflect Your Company's Values?

Even though recipients may receive these gifts personally, wherever they go, they have the potential to promote your company. Therefore, it's important to choose items that reflect the stories and values of your business.

If your company aims to minimize its environmental impact, it's wise to avoid plastic items. Instead, opt for environmentally friendly alternatives that align with your sustainability goals. Similarly, if your brand focuses on addressing practical challenges that individuals encounter in their lives, avoid impractical and gimmicky gifts that serve no real purpose.

By selecting gifts that align with your company's values and objectives, you can reinforce your brand message and create a positive impression among recipients. This approach ensures that the gifts not only serve as tokens of appreciation but also act as ambassadors for your business wherever they go.

How Crucial Is the Presentation?

Lastly, consider the presentation of the gift and whether it plays a role in captivating the intended recipient. The act of opening the package should be an exciting experience that adds to the recipient's anticipation.

When presenting the gift, it's important to express your feelings of appreciation. Use a beautiful box or bag to signify that you have gone the extra mile for your loyal clients and valued individuals.

By paying attention to the presentation, you enhance the overall experience for the recipient. It shows that you have put thought and effort into not only selecting the gift but also in creating a memorable moment when it is revealed. This attention to detail can leave a lasting impression and further convey your sincerity and gratitude.

What to Consider When Choosing Your Ideal Corporate Gifts

In this chapter, you will learn how to select appropriate gifts for both clients and colleagues. We will explore important factors to consider, as well as things to avoid, to help you choose the most suitable presents. Contrary to what you might think, it is not a difficult task. Showing your gratitude to your staff and customers simply requires some time and effort.

By understanding what makes a thoughtful gift for your employees, you can ensure that your gestures of appreciation are meaningful and truly valued.

A well-thought-out business gift requires careful consideration. The appropriate choice depends on various factors, including the characteristics of your target audience, your objectives, and your familiarity with the intended recipient. However, an exceptional business gift typically possesses certain qualities:

- Practicality: Opt for a gift that serves a practical purpose, as it will likely be more appreciated and frequently used.
- Thoughtfulness: Keep the recipient in mind while selecting a gift. Ensure that it is thoughtful and suitable for their preferences and needs.
- Personalization: Tailor the gift specifically to the recipient(s). Go beyond simply adding your company's logo to the wrapping paper. Consider incorporating elements such as the recipient's name, favorite color, specially designed packaging, or a heartfelt handwritten message. The best business gifts are crafted with the recipient in mind, making them more meaningful and memorable.

By considering these qualities, you can choose a business gift that is both practical and personalized, leaving a positive and lasting impression on the recipient.

The practice of giving gifts to business associates is rapidly evolving. Brands are striving to become more personal and accessible, which has led to a shift in how corporate gifts are approached. To begin, conduct thorough research to explore the top options for business presents.

Merely placing your company's name on a generic giveaway is no longer sufficient. It is essential to invest thought, planning, and individuality into every aspect of your gift-giving strategy. Corporate gifts have the potential to make a lasting impression that motivates employees, customers, or prospects to take action. The best corporate gift ideas will contribute to business growth and success through enhanced loyalty, increased engagement with the brand, product purchases, and positive word-of-mouth advertising.

But how can you come up with thoughtful gifts that truly resonate with your audience? In this section, we will guide you on how to select a corporate gift that deeply connects with recipients. Additionally, we will provide a curated list of fail-proof corporate gift ideas that never fail to impress.

As Ryan Howell, a psychologist at San Francisco State University, suggests, "The most significant aspect of gift exchange is demonstrating that you genuinely know and care about the recipient." By keeping this principle in mind, you can ensure that your corporate gifts convey a genuine sense of understanding and appreciation for the recipients.

Typically, this involves putting in the effort to personalize the gift for the recipient. According to Howell, individuals who aim to give meaningful gifts would not purchase the same gift for two friends, even if the friends are unaware of each other's gifts, wouldn't compare them, and have similar preferences.

The aspect of usability should not be overlooked. A study published in the Journal of Consumer Research in 2014 revealed that gift givers often overlook the usefulness of a gift to the recipient. In the study, participants preferred more expensive but less convenient options (like restaurant gift certificates) over cheaper but more practical options (such as a gift certificate for a closer, more affordable restaurant). However, the recipients of the gifts favored the more practical choice.

All of this might lead you to wonder, "What makes a good corporate gift?" Offering the right type of business gift can elicit a positive response, which is precisely why we give them. A gift has the potential to motivate someone to take the next step in a professional relationship.

Personalization and thoughtfulness can make a significant impact when it comes to gift-giving. By selecting highly personalized, useful, and valued items, you can make your brand more approachable to customers, clients, and employees. When you give gifts that are tailored to someone's interests or life situations, it really shows you care and know them well.

For instance, if a client often talks about their gardening hobby, sending a set of personalized gardening tools or a book on exotic plants can make them feel appreciated and understood. This personal touch can make your brand seem more relatable and warm.

On the other hand, for an employee who might be a coffee enthusiast, a subscription to a coffee of the month club or a custom-engraved coffee mug could be a delightful and useful gift. It not only caters to their interests but also shows that you notice and value these personal details.

These types of thoughtful gifts enhance the relationship, showing your clients and employees that there are real people behind your brand who listen and care. This can lead to stronger, more positive connections with your brand.

It's important to remember that people prefer to interact with other people, and corporate gifts can demonstrate that there is a human element behind your brand. It shows that you care.

Motivating employees goes beyond just giving pay raises. It's crucial to make each employee feel special and appreciated. Consider organizing parties to celebrate significant achievements by the company and individual team members. Giving gifts on work anniversaries can be a way to show appreciation for employees' hard work and dedication. Additionally, offering gifts when employees return to the workplace can help ease the transition into a new routine, especially for those who have been away. For employees working in a hybrid or remote setting, consider sending corporate care gifts to show your support and appreciation.

Lastly, don't underestimate the importance of new hire orientation. Introducing your approach to keeping new hires engaged from the beginning with a thoughtful token of appreciation can make a positive impression and set the tone for their experience with the company.

Corporate gift-giving holds a special significance among business professionals. It serves various purposes, including showing appreciation, inspiring action, and fostering collaboration. Apart from increasing a company's return on investment (ROI), it also helps build lasting relationships between the company's most valuable assets: its staff and its customers.

Business relationships can be strengthened when companies express gratitude by giving presents to their contacts. This practice has the potential to boost productivity and enhance employee satisfaction.

The giving company has the freedom to choose gifts based on what they believe will be most appreciated by the recipients. This can include a range of items such as expensive devices, laptop cases, snack foods, gift cards, and more.

To What End Do Businesses Provide Presents to Employees and Clients?

The purpose of giving gifts is to solidify a mutually beneficial connection between the giver and the recipient. Branded corporate gifts are an effective strategy for businesses to differentiate themselves, engage with customers, attract and retain employees, and strengthen relationships with business partners.

Corporate gift-giving has the potential to boost morale and enhance productivity in the workplace. It serves two primary purposes:

1. Building long-term commitment:
It establishes credibility with both existing and potential customers, distinguishing the company from competitors. By offering competitive services and benefits, businesses can prevent customers from considering switching providers.

2. Creating a pleasant work environment:
It fosters a positive workplace where employees feel valued for their contributions and are motivated to succeed. Companies can demonstrate their appreciation for hardworking employees by presenting them with branded corporate gifts such as laptop bags, watches, and other accessories.

When employees enjoy coming to work, they are more likely to perform well on a daily basis.

Expressing appreciation to both customers and employees is essential for businesses. Neglecting to value their contributions can lead to alienation and potentially drive them to seek opportunities elsewhere, which can be detrimental to the company.

However, on special occasions such as work anniversaries, birthdays, holidays, and more, a gift from the company can significantly boost morale.

You might be curious about the reasons behind this.

Corporate gifts contribute to uplifting the overall spirit within the company. Providing employees with corporate gifts is an effective way to enhance morale. It creates a win-win situation by fostering a relaxed and closer-knit environment while expressing gratitude for their hard work. Personalized corporate gifts, such as t-shirts and mugs with the company logo and each employee's name embroidered on them, have been shown to increase brand loyalty and instill a sense of pride in the workplace.

When employees feel satisfied, they are more inclined to go the extra mile and contribute to the overall success of the company. Personalized swag items like laptop bags, clothing, mugs, and more, adorned with the company's logo, serve as excellent promotional items.

Furthermore, giving branded corporate gifts to customers, suppliers, and staff is a gesture of respect that demonstrates appreciation for their loyalty to the company. In certain cultures, such as Japan, the act of presenting a gift holds great value, sometimes even surpassing the value of the gift itself.

With this in mind, businesses should exercise care when selecting corporate gifts for their employees and partners. The gifts should bring personal and professional benefits to the recipients.

For example, a frequent traveler would appreciate a corporate travel bag as it allows them to conveniently store their essentials in one place during their commutes.

Additionally, providing branded gear as a token of appreciation to B2B clients and staff helps differentiate your company from the competition, enhances brand recognition, and sets you apart. Simply offering verbal praise or recognition is often insufficient; employees also appreciate tangible rewards.

Publicly acknowledging the contributions of your employees and making efforts to recognize their efforts will be highly valued. The thoughtful selection of a gift shows that you took the time to consider their preferences. Even customers in the business-to-business sector can enjoy the enjoyable aspect of corporate gifts.

Treating customers well increases the likelihood of them doing business with the company again.

Gifts are an effective way to show appreciation to repeat buyers.

Sending a gift is a great strategy to express gratitude to loyal customers. It's not necessary to overwhelm them with gifts, but doing so demonstrates how much you value their business. Consequently, they will appreciate the gesture of a business gift.

Therefore, it's a win-win situation where you can show your appreciation and maintain a strong relationship with them.

Did you know that this strategy can also help boost sales?

Boosting sales and profits can be as simple as providing branded corporate gifts to both staff and customers, especially when the gifts are personalized based on the recipients' interests. Recognizing and appreciating their contributions will greatly impact their morale and motivation to excel in their roles within the organization. Their increased efforts will lead to higher sales for the company.

Similarly, customers will value the gift and recognize the benefits of continuing to do business with your organization. They will also see the value in the products or services offered and be more inclined to make future investments. This will create a perception of receiving excellent value for their money and increase their likelihood of returning as loyal customers.

The company or organization that gives out corporate gifts can expect a significant return on their investment, resulting in increased sales.

Corporate gift giving creates a positive and joyful atmosphere in the workplace. Boosting morale through the exchange of corporate gifts has been proven to be an effective strategy. Both customers and employees feel appreciated and develop a stronger sense of trust in the company's commitment to their needs.

When employees feel valued and appreciated, they are more motivated to exceed their goals. Investing in recognizing outstanding performance yields long-term profitability.

Customers are more likely to develop a connection with the company when they receive branded promotional items. This fosters a greater willingness to engage in business with the company.

Additionally, this helps raise awareness and generate positive word-of-mouth about the company. Sending gifts to business connections is an excellent way to enhance brand recognition and exposure. These gifts can be tailored to the recipient's preferences and can be personalized with their name, the company's logo, and other artwork. When these gifts are used in public, they serve as ambassadors for the company, spreading positive impressions and reflecting the company's positive work environment. Examples of such gifts include branded tote bags, coffee cups, and more.

Whenever the recipients use the gifts, they will have a positive association with the organization. Branded business gifts can include items of clothing, accessories like umbrellas, and drinkware, which serve as effective examples.

To enhance your company's visibility, consider giving corporate gifts to your staff and customers as the new year approaches.

Distributing branded promotional gifts is one of the most cost-effective forms of advertising, yielding a quick return on investment. Businesses should consider stocking up on high-quality branded merchandise at wholesale prices to show appreciation for their staff, vendors, and customers on special occasions. In the long run, these tangible presents serve as effective advertising because recipients will remember the organization whenever they use them.

Corporate gifts are an excellent advertising tool as recipients are likely to use the items. This not only showcases the organization's dedication but also has the potential to attract new customers.

Giving corporate gifts to employees and customers strengthens professional relationships. The objective of any gift should be to highlight the unique qualities of the recipient and show appreciation for them. A foolproof approach is to provide a gift tailored specifically to their tastes.

Companies can demonstrate their care for employees as individuals, in addition to clients and workers, by giving them meaningful gifts that hold personal significance.

Gift-giving also creates an opportunity for positive discussions. Companies that use corporate gifts to maintain communication with customers and employees are often praised for fostering open lines of communication. When employees are rewarded with corporate gifts, they develop trust in the organization and are more likely to provide constructive feedback. This input is essential for the company's growth and improvement.

The key takeaway from our discussion is the importance of thoughtful consideration when dealing with corporate gifts. I hope that you now have a deeper understanding of the significance of gifts in the business world.

After all, any company striving for greatness relies on strong team cohesion and fruitful business partnerships. Show your business contacts that you care by giving them something special on important occasions.

Corporate Gifting Best Practices

So, now that we have discussed corporate gifts, their purpose, and their impact, let's delve into how to excel at giving them. What makes a good gift, and how should you present it?

Corporate gifts can be utilized in various contexts to show appreciation for your staff. It's important not to limit employee recognition to traditional occasions like holidays. Keeping your staff engaged requires ongoing effort throughout the year. Team members feel more valued when their achievements, both professional and personal, are acknowledged.

There are some well-known secrets to giving memorable gifts, and they all have stories behind them. From our experience, we know we have something special on our hands when a gift accomplishes one or more of the following:

- Conveys the message that you have taken the time to understand the recipient and appreciate what is important to them.
- Reflects unique qualities about you or your relationship with the recipient.
- Marks a significant and memorable moment in the recipient's life.
- Transforms into something more than just a gift for the recipient.

When Can You Give Away Your Corporate Gifts?

It's essential to plan your gift-giving in a way that aligns with your company's resources and avoids undue stress. Here are a few special occasions that call for thoughtful business gifts:

- Holidays, including international ones (such as Christmas, Easter, Chinese New Year, etc.)
- Workplace milestones and anniversaries
- End of the fiscal year
- Achievement of performance targets (e.g., highest sales in a month)
- Corporate events and customer-centered gatherings
- Ceremonies recognizing award recipients

Remember to consider that some of your customers may come from different cultural backgrounds, each with their own expectations regarding business gifts. For example, in Japan, there are specific norms and etiquette for giving and receiving gifts in a business context.

Understanding as much as possible about your international clients or coworkers before giving a gift can greatly benefit your company. Providing a gift that reflects their personality and interests is ideal. At the very least, you can take inspiration from the types of items commonly given as business gifts in their respective countries.

In today's competitive landscape, it's more important than ever to stay ahead of the competition. With new companies emerging both online and offline every day, there's always the risk of customers considering switching to a service provider that offers superior service, products, or experiences.

One effective way to differentiate your company from the competition is by regularly giving freebies to your customers. This not only shows that you value your customers but also demonstrates your willingness to go the extra mile for them. As word spreads about your exceptional offerings, you will naturally attract a growing customer base.

Promotional items make excellent freebies as they incentivize clients and foster loyalty towards your business. Giving corporate gifts to customers and employees is a powerful way to express appreciation and encourage loyalty.

These gifts can be given at any time of the year, but the holiday season is particularly suitable. Additionally, they can be presented as tokens of appreciation for significant occasions, such as work anniversaries (e.g., fifth, tenth, twentieth, etc.).

Acknowledging the departure of a coworker? Saying goodbye can be tough for everyone involved, but a considerate farewell gift can help lighten the mood. Raise a glass and bid farewell to the staff member you'll miss with one of our exceptional corporate gift boxes.

It's important for businesses of all sizes to show their gratitude to departing employees by offering a personal gesture of respect. When the separation process is handled with care and employees have a positive experience, they are more likely to look back on their time with the company fondly. A beautiful gift box can contribute to achieving that goal.

Gifts given to employees by companies should be meaningful and appreciated. The goal of corporate gift giving can be achieved through careful consideration of the items, messaging, and packaging selected. The following tips will help you choose the most suitable business gifts:

1. Put in the effort and plan ahead. While we always emphasize the importance of planning ahead to our customers, it becomes even more crucial in the future. Disruptions in the global supply chain, such as price increases, stockouts, and shipping delays, are expected to continue. By planning early, setting a budget now, and placing orders well in advance, you will have an easier time finding the perfect gifts for your recipients.

2. Don't limit your planning to major holidays. While it is customary to show gratitude to business associates during the last quarter of the year, unexpected gifts can often be the most cherished. By keeping track of your staff's and customers' achievements throughout the year, you can express your appreciation with more thoughtful gifts on various occasions.

By following these guidelines, you can ensure that your corporate gifts are well-received and make a lasting impression on your recipients.

Different Corporate Gifting Strategies

Corporate gifting can take various forms, with two main categories: tangible gifts and intangible gifts.

Tangible gifts are the most common type of corporate presents, typically physical items that are often branded with the recipient's name and the company's name. However, corporate gifts don't have to be limited to products alone.

Intangible gifts, on the other hand, offer a unique and cutting-edge approach to showing appreciation. These gifts focus on experiences rather than physical items. They can bring greater joy to the lives of selected recipients and strengthen their positive relationship with your company. However, it's worth noting that giving a wonderful gift card is always a safe and appreciated choice.

If you truly want to stand out and leave a lasting impression on the recipient, opting for a memorable intangible gift can be an excellent choice. Such gifts go beyond traditional material items and provide an unforgettable experience or opportunity.

The most impactful gifts are often the ones that create lasting memories rather than simply providing material possessions.

Research conducted by the University of Pennsylvania's Wharton School suggests that giving experiences as gifts, such as concert tickets or zoo memberships, can foster a closer connection between the giver and recipient compared to tangible objects. Surprisingly, the shared experience is not even necessary for this increased sense of connection to occur.

A recent study co-authored by researchers from Washington University in St. Louis and Seoul National University further supports the idea that giving experiences, rather than material items, is a powerful way to show appreciation. The study suggests that people may underestimate the value of experience gifts, possibly due to hesitations about offering such gifts to individuals with whom they have a less familiar relationship.

For example, consider a situation where you know a coworker enjoys live music. Instead of buying them a new set of headphones, you might buy tickets to a concert by their favorite band. This kind of gift not only provides a fun night out, but it also creates memories that can outlast any material item.

Similarly, if you have a coworker or client who loves cooking, instead of giving them a cookbook, you could gift them a cooking class with a local chef. This experience not only enhances their skills but also gives them a chance to enjoy something they love in a new way.

These examples show how choosing the right type of gift—focusing on what the person will actually enjoy and remember—can make all the difference. It's about understanding the recipients' interests and turning them into special experiences that show how much you appreciate them.

Furthermore, according to the findings of researcher Thomas Gilovich, providing someone with a unique and unforgettable experience is a guaranteed way to bring happiness. Even if a recipient had anticipated receiving a tangible gift, receiving an experience instead can still lead to satisfaction. On the other hand, if someone had anticipated an experience gift but received a physical object instead, they are likely to be disappointed.

In addition to physical gifts and experiences, another meaningful way to show appreciation is by making a contribution in someone's honor.

Research suggests that happiness can be enhanced by donating to those in need or supporting causes that hold personal significance. A study conducted by Harvard Business School researchers in 2009 highlighted a positive relationship between happiness and charitable giving.

The satisfaction derived from making donations can be amplified when it strengthens connections with others. Research published in the International Journal of Happiness and Development in 2013 found that individuals tend to experience greater happiness when they make a gift through a friend or family member, as opposed to making an anonymous donation.

Now, let's explore some gift ideas that you can consider for your employees:

Personalized Jackets for Employees

Offering your staff personalized company jackets is an excellent way to enhance team morale and promote your business. Branded jackets, with the option for personalization, can create a stronger connection with your employees, fostering their appreciation for their work. As a thoughtful gesture, consider embroidering a meaningful phrase, the employee's name, or a nickname on each jacket and presenting it to them.

Personalized Electronics

Branded tech gadgets make for fantastic corporate gifts, suitable for both remote and on-site workers. Employees will appreciate gifts that streamline their daily work routines, especially with the increasing popularity of virtual meetings as a means of collaboration. Consider practical items such as branded power banks or earphones featuring your company's branding. These items ensure that employees stay connected and energized throughout their workday.

Branded Luggage

Company-branded bags or backpacks are not only practical and versatile Christmas gifts for employees but also complement the other gift ideas mentioned earlier. Imagine durable bags that can withstand outdoor activities like camping and hiking while still providing ample space for a laptop and other work or travel essentials.

Customer Appreciation Giveaways

Giving gifts to clients is not only a kind gesture but also a strategic one. It's important to demonstrate to key customers that you value them and their business, and providing them with a gift shows that you are willing to invest in them. When selecting gifts for customers, it's crucial to avoid generic options. Put thought into the gift and make it unique by including a handwritten note or custom logo. Go the extra mile by offering presents that are tailored to their individual passions and preferences.

Here are some of our preferred gift categories for customers, which can be customized to suit your specific clientele:

Food Gifts

Delighting clients with delicious and unique food offerings is a great way to impress them and strengthen your relationship. Engaging a customer's sense of smell, taste, and touch can create a memorable and meaningful experience. Combine the lasting power of your brand with the pleasure of food for maximum impact. Consider options such as snack baskets, assorted coffee and tea sets, or even a gourmet bread basket.

Personalized Blankets

Clients will appreciate receiving a personalized blanket as it can be used anywhere. Additionally, they are easy to customize with your company's logo or other designs. Fleece and sherpa blankets are two examples that fit the bill.

Products for the Hybrid Workplace

Since many individuals now split their time between the office and working from home, gifts that cater to the hybrid work environment are practical and well-received. Think of items that seamlessly transition from the workplace to a home office setup. Finding the perfect gifts for customers may require some creativity, but high-quality solutions like a wireless charging mouse pad or a writing pad can be both innovative and useful.

Corporate Gift Boxes

Corporate gift boxes are a wonderful way to express gratitude to employees and clients during the holiday season. They combine a thoughtful selection of items with a special message and elegant packaging. Another option for reaching colleagues or customers who are located far away is to send gift baskets directly to their homes.

If you're planning to send a business gift box before the holidays, it's important to start organizing early. The entire process, from conceptualizing the design of the gift box to going through the printing process, typically takes around seven weeks. Additionally, consider shipping costs and size restrictions if you're planning to deliver a custom package.

For great holiday gift ideas for your company's employees, consider the following:

Personalized Drinkware

Personalized drinkware is a versatile gift that can be enjoyed by individuals of all ages. Its compact size makes it ideal for presentation in a high-end gift box. There are various options for personalization, including features for both hot and cold beverages, making it easy to choose the perfect gift. Insulated tumblers that can accommodate both hot and cold liquids are currently popular, especially as more environmentally friendly versions become available.

Custom Logo Coolers

We've observed a growing trend in the use of high-end lunch containers such as insulated coolers and branded bento boxes. These container-based meals help employees prioritize healthy eating habits, which is a topic of increasing importance. These items are also compact enough to be included in a gift box and can be paired with a variety of other gifts.

Branded Product Bundles

Purchasing a gift bundle is a convenient way to fill a corporate gift box. Many upscale brands offer pre-made sets, eliminating the need to search for complementary items. Combine more practical items with more indulgent ones, such as savory snack packs or gourmet chocolates. You can also unleash your creativity by pairing specialty cocktail mixers with elegant glassware. Adding a personal touch will ensure that your workplace gift is even more appreciated.

High-End Promotional Items

Not all customers are the same, and it's important to recognize and reward your top clients who contribute the most to your business. High-end corporate gifts are typically reserved for a select group of the company's most valued clients. The following categories of items can serve as premium giveaways.

Drawing inspiration from popular and reputable retail brands is a good starting point for these products. Another option for delivering a high-quality gift is to create a gift bundle. For example, you can include food gift baskets packaged in a branded cooler or a cocktail gift set complete with branded glassware and premium cocktail mixes. You can choose from a variety of pre-made gift sets or create your own by carefully selecting items that align with your recipients' preferences.

Corporate Donations

Making a donation in a client's name can be a powerful and meaningful corporate gift, especially for clients who value social responsibility. This form of giving not only benefits the recipient organization but also aligns your company with charitable efforts, enhancing your brand's image.

Whether it's a financial contribution to a non-profit that resonates with the client's personal beliefs or sponsorship of an event they care deeply about, corporate donations show thoughtfulness beyond typical gift-giving. It allows your company to make a positive impact in the community while honoring the relationship with your client. Choose a cause or organization that reflects shared values between your company and the client to make this gift particularly impactful.

Inexpensive Gifts

Giving a meaningful corporate gift doesn't have to break the bank. Even a small token of appreciation can carry great significance. There are still ways to show your appreciation to employees or customers even when you have a tight budget. Opting for gifts that provide experiences while being personalized can be a great option for cost-conscious individuals.

Here are a few suggestions:

1. Hot Chocolate Bombs are a creative twist on a classic present. When the chocolate "bomb" is dropped into a mug of steaming milk, it magically dissolves and creates a delicious hot chocolate drink. This gift can be particularly enjoyed by recipients with young children.

2. A bamboo cutting board is a practical and eco-friendly gift that is both simple and elegant. It is a versatile kitchen tool that will be appreciated by the recipient

3. Wireless chargers are a useful and stylish gift that everyone can benefit from. The practicality of the gift, combined with its distinctive design, will be highly appreciated by the recipients. Your brand will be prominently displayed with a complimentary full-color imprint, adding a touch of luxury to the gift.

Presents With a Purpose

Today's consumers have higher expectations when it comes to the brands they support. They seek out businesses that align with their values and demonstrate a commitment to the community. By investing in and giving away items that contribute to a charitable cause, you can show your customers and clients that your company remains focused on its broader mission. Many influential companies offer a wide range of products that support various initiatives.

One example is insulated tumblers. Some brands allocate a portion of their profits to initiatives promoting safe drinking water, environmental sustainability, and community well-being.

In the production of their products, many modern brands utilize eco-friendly materials such as bamboo, wheat straw, and recycled cotton. Additionally, a portion of the proceeds often goes to support environmental organizations worldwide.

For instance, if you purchase gifts from Basecamp, a company known for its high-quality bags, coolers, and drinkware, the company donates these items to organizations that assist injured soldiers. Basecamp has a special connection to the Wounded Warrior Project, which helps injured military veterans transition to civilian life.

Numerous companies offer trendy water containers that serve a dual purpose of providing a practical product and supporting the global fight for clean water. With each purchase, these companies contribute to the provision of wells and other sustainable clean water solutions for communities in need worldwide.

Promo Items for Prospective Buyers

Prospects can be effectively nurtured throughout the sales funnel by incorporating thoughtful and personalized gifts. When prospecting for sales, it is important to carefully select and provide gifts to potential clients. The right gift can establish an authentic relationship with clients even before the sales process begins. As you continue to nurture them through the funnel, this bond will be remembered and appreciated.

When choosing sales prospecting gifts, take into consideration the recipient's preferences, needs, and interests. Here are a few suggestions to help you get started, and don't forget to customize the message with the prospect's name or the company's logo.

A Stainless-Steel Tumbler is a practical gift that customers will appreciate. With its unique built-in straw and high-quality construction, it keeps beverages cool throughout the day. You can add a custom imprint, such as a company logo, to personalize the tumbler.

A Bento Lunch Box is a convenient gift for clients, whether they are at the office or on the go. Its eco-friendly design, combined with a bamboo cutting board that serves as a cover, makes it both practical and thoughtful.

Consider a compact vacuum cleaner that can be used to clean desktops and other flat surfaces. Its innovative design will impress customers and provide them with a useful tool they may not have encountered before.

Branded bottles are an excellent way to support a good cause while enjoying a high-quality product. Designed with portability in mind, these bottles have a simple, leak-proof, single-wall construction with a screw-on lid. Personalizing the bottle with a prospect's name shows that you care about them, making the gesture more impactful.

Wireless chargers and branded power banks are also impressive and practical options to include in your corporate gift selection. A branded power bank, in particular, is a reliable choice as it is practical enough to make a strong impression on potential clients without exceeding your budget.

Giving gifts as a company can generate conversations and create a buzz. People naturally have a tendency to reciprocate favors when they are bestowed upon them. If you want to elevate your professional connection with someone, consider giving them a thoughtful gift.

Corporate Gift Guides

There are advantages and disadvantages to using corporate gift guides. On the positive side, corporate gift guides can be a valuable resource for finding appropriate gift ideas in the business world and staying updated on corporate gift trends. However, on the negative side, some corporate gift guides may be too generic and not always relevant to the business context. Additionally, following corporate gift guides can be expensive. When utilizing corporate gift guides, it is important to approach them strategically. For instance, they can be used to identify trends in corporate gifting or to discover gifts that align with the professional environment.

It is worth noting that corporate gift guides have not extensively explored the realm of corporate relationships. Many existing gift guides are structured around the recipient's personal relationship to the giver (e.g., "gifts for Dad"), shared interests (e.g., "gifts for animal lovers"), or specific occasions. Consequently, there is often a lack of focus on corporate relationships in these guides.

Nevertheless, corporate gift guides can still be valuable, particularly for new companies that are just starting out. A well-curated corporate gift guide can alleviate the stress of brainstorming, planning, and acquiring the right gifts. It can streamline the planning process and provide guidance in the right direction.

When carefully curated, corporate gift guides can also address the distinctions between regular clients and highly esteemed clients. They can assist in determining the most suitable gifts for veteran patrons who have made significant investments in your business.

One often overlooked advantage of using corporate gift guides is their ability to help emerging companies identify solid gifting trends. By doing so, these guides can alleviate the stress associated with corporate gifting and provide a solid foundation for companies entering this realm. They offer inspiration and insights into the practices of other companies, allowing businesses to choose whether to innovate or follow established trends.

However, it's important to note that corporate gifting is still a relatively new field, and there is room for further progress. This can result in many gift guides feeling generic and mainstream. As we have explored in this book, corporate gifting involves various factors and can be challenging at times. As a result, you may not find wildly unique ideas in corporate gift guides. Nevertheless, these guides serve as a valuable resource to stimulate your own creativity and generate excellent gifting ideas.

Cost is a significant consideration when using gift guides. Some guides can be expensive, but each company should conduct its own cost-benefit analysis to determine the value they can derive from using them. For new businesses looking to enter the corporate gifting realm, the simplicity and inspiration provided by these guides can be beneficial.

As corporate gifting continues to gain traction in the business world, we can anticipate that corporate gift guides will become increasingly important and integrated into corporate culture. In other words, they are on the rise and are here to stay.

A Real-World Example of Transforming Event Presence Through Strategic Gifting: CCMG's Success Story

In the competitive landscape of industry events, standing out from the crowd can be a significant challenge, especially for businesses in sectors often perceived as less exciting, such as accounting and finance. This case study demonstrates how strategic corporate gifting can transform a company's presence at such events, turning a potentially overlooked booth into a center of attention and engagement.

At the 2022 Congress of Executives of Early Childhood Centers and Daycares in St-Hyacinthe, Quebec, CCMG, a Canadian CPA firm, faced the challenge of differentiating themselves in a sea of exhibitors. The event, which brings together directors of Early Childhood Centers and Daycares from Montreal and surrounding areas, presented a unique opportunity for businesses serving this sector. However, CCMG needed to overcome the hurdle of attracting attention in an industry not typically associated with excitement or innovation.

Recognizing the potential value of each new client, which could represent a four to five-digit annual revenue increase, CCMG sought to maximize their return on investment for their booth participation. Moving beyond traditional giveaways like branded pens or water bottles, CCMG collaborated on a more impactful approach to corporate gifting.

The strategy centered around the use of premium, highly scented, three-wick candles as the primary gift. These candles were not just any ordinary promotional item; they were carefully designed to align with CCMG's brand, featuring their logo and an inviting message on the label. The vibrant color of the wax was chosen to match CCMG's logo, creating a visually striking display that drew immediate attention to their booth.

What set this gifting strategy apart was the engagement requirement tied to receiving the gift. Attendees had to provide a business card and listen to CCMG's pitch to receive the free candle. This approach ensured that each gift given resulted in a meaningful interaction and potential lead for CCMG.

The execution of this strategy involved meticulous preparation. Branded candles were produced with careful attention to quality and visual appeal. The booth was set up to prominently display these eye-catching gifts, and CCMG team members were thoroughly briefed on the engagement strategy. To ensure the strategy's success and gather real-time insights, a representative flew to Canada to observe its implementation firsthand.

The results of this innovative approach were remarkable. Throughout the event, attendees were seen carrying the distinctive candles, effectively turning them into mobile advertisements for CCMG. Conversations overheard at the event indicated that attendees were actively seeking out CCMG's booth specifically for these unique gifts. This word-of-mouth marketing extended CCMG's reach beyond direct interactions, prompting inquiries from individuals who hadn't even visited their booth.

Over the two-day event, CCMG distributed most of their prepared candles, each representing a potential new business connection. The ROI calculation was straightforward yet powerful: acquiring just one new client from the event would be sufficient not only to break even but to profit from the corporate gift investment. Additionally, any remaining candles could be repurposed for employee appreciation, extending the value of the investment beyond the event itself.

This case study highlights several key principles for effective corporate gifting at industry events:

1. Premium gifts stand out: High-quality, unique gifts can differentiate a company even in industries traditionally seen as "less exciting".

2. Strategic distribution enhances engagement: Requiring a business card and brief interaction maximizes the value of each gift given.

3. Visual impact matters: Matching gift colors to brand colors reinforces brand identity and recognition.

4. Word-of-mouth power: Distinctive gifts can create a buzz at events, extending reach beyond direct interactions.

5. ROI focus: When the value of a single new client is high, investing in premium gifts can quickly become profitable.

6. Cross-event application: Successful strategies can be adapted and applied to various industry events.

7. Personal observation yields insights: Being present at the event allowed for real-time strategy assessment and future improvements.

By thoughtfully implementing this strategic gifting approach, CCMG was able to transform their presence at the industry event. They turned what could have been an overlooked booth into a center of attention and engagement, creating meaningful connections with potential high-value clients. This real-world example illustrates the power of creative thinking in corporate gifting to overcome industry-specific challenges and maximize the impact of event participation.

CHAPTER 4

Business Gift Giving: Dos and Don'ts

You've made the decision to use corporate gifts as a means to expand your business, but you're unsure of the best approach. You may be wondering what gifts would truly impress the recipient.

In many professional settings, giving and receiving gifts is a common practice. However, it's crucial to exercise caution, as gifts from a company can lead to unfavorable outcomes if not handled properly.

You may have questioned the appropriate behavior when sending a corporate gift to a business associate, customer, or partner. While the act of giving a gift is highly appreciated, it's essential to consider the guidelines of corporate gift-giving etiquette to ensure that your gift is received with gratitude.

Throughout this book, the terms "business gift," "corporate gift," and "promotional gift" will be used interchangeably to refer to items exchanged between businesses or between an organization and a client. This is not meant to downplay the significance of their technical distinctions, but rather to emphasize the common elements of the gift-giving process.

Distributing corporate gifts is an excellent strategy for establishing and strengthening relationships with your target audience. These gifts often take the form of branded promotional items.

While many companies appreciate receiving gifts and understand that you are promoting your brand and services, it's important to be aware that some individuals may perceive your gesture as an attempt to bribe them or engage in underhanded sales tactics.

Although it may seem that way to some, your intention is not to disguise any ulterior motives. The exchange of promotional gifts is a customary practice in business, with the original gift being viewed as a simple act of goodwill.

While donations are acceptable, it's important to always be considerate and avoid using money as a means to manipulate or gain advantage. Whether a gift is seen as genuine or as a bribe depends on the specific circumstances.

Now, let's explore how to discern whether the "promotional gifts" you're providing to another company could be perceived as an attempt to bribe them.

When Doing Business, What Actions Are Considered Bribery?

When an individual engages in dishonest behavior with the intention of receiving favorable treatment in return, it is referred to as a bribe.

The term "bribe" can encompass a range of actions, from minor infractions that people may do without much thought to major unlawful offenses that are expressly prohibited by law or policy. For example, bribing a public official in order to gain an advantage is a clear example of this.

On the other hand, a gift is given without any expectation of compensation. It is freely offered and should not be accompanied by any implicit or explicit requests for something in return.

When sending promotional presents to another company, it's important to focus on showcasing your brand and introducing yourself in a professional manner. The purpose should not be to use the gift as an opportunity to advertise your services.

Avoid over-explaining yourself or trying to grovel your way into anything. Instead, present a meaningful token that reflects your values and goodwill. The intention should never be to provide any form of bribe or engage in any unethical behavior.

When Doing Business, What is the Proper Protocol for Giving Gifts?

How you and the recipient should behave during gift exchanges can vary, but it's crucial to maintain professionalism at all times.

To avoid giving the impression that you don't value your potential business partners, collaborators, and customers, it's important to avoid being too casual in your communications.

Since you are conducting business, it is advisable to follow business-like gift-giving protocols and guidelines.

In this guide, you will find some do's and don'ts when it comes to sending corporate gifts.

Do:

- Maintain good taste: Including your company's logo on a gift can showcase your professionalism. A well-designed business gift with subtle logos in the appropriate company colors is effective.
- Express gratitude and consideration: Consider sending a modest and relevant gift to specific contacts at other firms on holidays or special occasions as a gesture of gratitude and care.
- Choose a gift that will be appreciated by everyone: Snacks and treats are always a safe option, but any small token of appreciation will suffice. When making a selection, aim for something that has broad appeal.
- Provide relevant and useful information: If you are familiar with the organization or the individuals you are gifting, try to choose

something more personalized. This is particularly valuable if you have recently established a connection or bonded with them.

Don't:

- Accidentally damage the reputation of your company. Avoid potentially unprofessional elements such as oversized logos, clashing colors, or last-minute changes. Keeping things simple is key, as the gift represents your business.
- Show favoritism. If you work closely with multiple individuals at the recipient's company, ensure that you purchase comparable or identical gifts for each of them. Avoid creating the perception of favoritism within the organization.
- Overwhelm recipients with advertisements. The primary goal of a corporate gift should be to express gratitude, not to promote your business. Avoid giving gifts that could be misconstrued as advertising.
- Oversell. Steer clear of overly promotional items. Your gift should not sound like a sales pitch but rather convey genuine kindness.
- Give the impression of bribery. It's crucial to consider how to reward employees without creating the wrong perception. Corporate gifts are appropriate after successful meetings, agreements, holidays, or other significant events.

Choosing the perfect gift for coworkers and customers can be challenging. Striking the right balance between the ideal item and adhering to company gift standards can be tricky.

By following these guidelines, you will be able to select a suitable, well-received, and memorable gift for all the right reasons, whether you shop at traditional stores, peruse catalogs, or browse online.

Let's discuss some other key points to keep in mind.

Adhere to the Company's Policies

Ensure that you are familiar with your company's policies regarding gifts for staff. Some businesses have specific regulations in place. If you require clarification, reach out to your customers or the company's HR department.

Don't Forget About the Customer

Take the time to understand the interests and preferences of your clientele in order to provide better service. Your customer may have a favorite beverage or snack. Seek assistance from a coworker or assistant if needed. Give a gift that is as memorable as your business.

Consider the Price Tag

Be mindful of the potential negative consequences of giving a cheap gift. On the other hand, a lavish gift may make the recipient uncomfortable or go against business policies. Educate yourself on the subject. If you aim to impress a client with a business gift, nothing can be more embarrassing than having it rejected.

Reconsider Branding the Gift With Your Company Logo

Ensure that the product meets high standards and that your brand is tastefully presented to avoid appearing overly promotional.

Act in a Respectful Manner

It is important to be mindful of potential misinterpretations when giving gifts to individuals of the opposite sex. To avoid any personal implications, it is best to avoid gifts that may be seen as too intimate.

Consider the Recipient's Sense of Humor

What one person finds funny, another may find offensive. Before giving a humorous gift, make sure you understand your customer's sense of humor to avoid any unintended offense.

Make a Charitable Contribution

Research the client's charitable preferences and select an organization they already support. This benefits both the cause and all parties involved. It eliminates the concern of receiving unwanted gifts while supporting a worthy cause. Including a handwritten message or gift card to acknowledge the contribution adds a personal touch.

Pay Attention to Visual Presentation

Ensure that your gift is well-wrapped and aesthetically pleasing, following the appropriate holiday theme. The presentation of the gift, including the wrapping paper, is part of the overall experience. Consider including a handwritten message or notifying the recipient of a charitable donation made on their behalf.

Be Considerate With Group Gifts

If you plan to send food to a client's workplace, ensure that there is enough for everyone. Starting a food battle or causing conflicts over limited resources is not desirable during the holidays.

Keep Your Ultimate Goal in Mind

The purpose of giving gifts is to express gratitude and be remembered in business relationships. It is also an excellent way to show appreciation to your supporters. Remember your objective when selecting and giving gifts.

Exercise Caution With Office Gift Exchanges

Even with good intentions, gift exchanges among coworkers can lead to misunderstandings and friction. Establish clear ground rules to ensure a smooth and comfortable gift-giving experience in the office.

There Needs to Be Agreement Among Coworkers or Employees on the Preferred Approach

Will everyone bring a gift for each other? Will there be a Secret Santa-style drawing where one gift is purchased for everyone? Should there be a pre-determined price range? It is crucial to address these questions well in advance of the holidays. Considering the individual financial situations of each person is important, especially in challenging economic times. No one should feel obligated to participate if it is a financial burden.

Is It Necessary to Get a Gift for the Boss?

The employer, who likely earns a higher salary than you, should be the one responsible for buying holiday gifts for their employees, not the other way around. However, team members may choose to contribute together to purchase a gift for the boss as a group. In such cases, it is important to stick to a reasonable budget and avoid giving the impression of trying to gain favor by spending a lot of money.

What if You Want to Give Something Special to a Select Group of Close Coworkers?

In such cases, it is best to give the gifts outside of the workplace to avoid favoritism. Managers should not show preferential treatment to certain employees when recognizing their efforts. While the gifts don't have to be identical, they should be of similar value to ensure fairness.

Remember to Express Gratitude

Show gratitude twice: first when opening the gift and again in a thank-you message. Acknowledging and appreciating the thoughtful gesture is important in maintaining professional relationships.

Handling Gifts Received From Other Companies

Professionalism should be maintained when dealing with gifts from other companies, as reciprocity can be uncertain. It is essential to handle such situations with knowledge and tact. These guidelines and suggestions are just the beginning when it comes to the art of professional gift-giving.

Should You Start by Making Contact?

Sending a promotional gift to a person or company with whom you have had no prior interaction is not always an appropriate practice.

However, if you do decide to send a gift, make sure to include a message introducing yourself and clarifying the purpose of the gift. Don't forget to provide your contact details as well.

It's generally a good idea to initiate conversation first, whether it's in person or through various technological channels. This shows that you are not simply bombarding them with advertisements and are genuinely interested in establishing a connection.

What is the Proper Way to Offer Business Presents?

Giving a business gift is an opportunity to showcase not only what you do but how you do it. The presentation and thoughtfulness behind the gift often speak louder than the item itself.

Avoid simply delivering a package with unwrapped items. Put effort into the presentation to make it visually appealing and show that you value the recipient.

Take the extra step to ensure that the packaging is appropriate for the size of the gift. Send your marketing gift in a way that you would appreciate receiving one.

Demonstrating attention to detail reflects well on your company's ethos and communicates the quality of your work.

Is It Ethical to Receive Gifts When Doing Business With Another Company?

Accepting business gifts from others can be appropriate and ethical. The ethical question lies not in giving gifts but in receiving them.

These practices align with accepted norms in the corporate world.

Sending a thank-you note or card after receiving a gift is standard practice and a good way to show appreciation. However, it's important to avoid getting drawn into a bribery scenario.

Corporate Gift Giving: Guidelines for Compliant Policies

Choosing an appropriate corporate gift can indeed be challenging, whether you're responsible for purchasing a gift or simply looking to show appreciation to your staff. Questions like "What is fitting?" or "How much should I spend?" may arise, and it can be difficult to determine what your colleagues expect from you.

However, worry not! By following these tried-and-true guidelines, you can select and present the perfect corporate gift:

Ensure compliance with the law.

Gifting is subject to strict regulations in various fields, and giving the wrong gift to the wrong person can land you in a difficult situation. Laws define what constitutes an acceptable gift and what does not.

Acceptable Gifts:

- Promotional items with the company's branding but no significant value
- Shared meals between the giver and the recipient
- Perishable presents
- Gifts that adhere to legal and business gift restrictions
- Gifts that have been authorized by a manager

Inappropriate Gifts:

- Gifts for public servants
- Multiple gifts
- Requests for donations
- Gifts that exceed their nominal value

Absolutely Unacceptable Gifts:

- Extravagant presents
- Premium gifts that grossly exceed the company's threshold
- Gifts that can influence business decisions
- Attempting to buy favor with government officials through gifts
- Gifts that could be perceived as bribes
- Cash donations

It's important to be aware of these guidelines and to choose gifts that align with them in order to maintain professionalism and ethical standards in corporate gifting.

Always consult with a compliance officer or HR representative before making a purchase to ensure the appropriateness of the gift you intend to give.

When it comes to corporate gifts, prioritize recipients who are out-side your organization, such as customers, prospects, service providers, or business partners. Giving presents to these individuals is an effective way to strengthen relationships and potentially attract new customers.

The recipient of the gift matters less than the nature of the gift itself. Opt for a low-risk option, such as a small item, and ensure that the gift and any accompanying notes are not tied to specific events.

If you're unsure of what to send, a modest branded token can go a long way. Remember that "small" does not equate to "cheap." An impersonal token of gratitude, such as a branded gift, is often appreciated.

Choosing gifts for employees or colleagues can pose a challenge. If you're responsible for selecting a workplace gift, opt for something that everyone can use. It's safest to provide the same gift to all staff members, regardless of their rank.

If you wish to deviate from the standard approach, ensure it aligns with a well-thought-out giving plan that has been documented. It is acceptable for businesses to reward long-serving employees with more extravagant gifts, but make sure the gifts are comparable in cost and na-ture. Take a moment to evaluate whether your gift choices are reasonable before finalizing any decisions. If necessary, be willing to reconsider and start afresh.

When purchasing gifts for individual team members or colleagues, especially if they are not your supervisors, it is advisable to give the gift outside of the workplace setting.

You should consider not giving a present to an individual if you don't have interactions with them outside of work. However, a small card or token of appreciation is often appropriate when shopping for a boss or superior.

Maintain consistency in the quality and price range of the gifts you provide to your staff. Additionally, ensure that you don't exclude anyone. It would be impolite to only purchase gifts for a few people on the team if you intended to give gifts to everyone.

Always consider whether a gift may offend the recipient before giv-ing it. Will the gift cause any issues with staff morale? Is it appropriate to give this gift in a work setting? Do you have any concerns that it could be perceived as bribery, favoritism, or anything undesirable? If you have any reservations about the gift being appreciated, it's best not to give it.

Regardless of the recipient, if a gift is overly lavish, it can create the wrong impression. Someone you are doing business with or trying to influence may interpret it as an attempt to buy their favor. The recipient of an extravagant gift may feel indebted to you or think that you are showing favoritism based on their efforts.

To avoid embarrassment, keep your business gifts simple and practical.

Lastly, always consult the company's manual for answers to your questions. If you don't have a corporate handbook or it doesn't address gift-giving, reach out to the human resources department. They are there to provide guidance in such situations.

Instead of dealing with an issue after it has already occurred, your HR department would prefer to address your concerns and help you avoid problems in the first place.

While people usually have good intentions when giving gifts, it's better to be safe than sorry. A well-intentioned gift can easily become a source of bias, ethical violations, or workplace conflicts if the recipient doesn't respond appropriately.

However, this shouldn't dampen your holiday spirit! The ability to give thoughtful gifts is a skill that can be quickly developed. Moreover, studies have shown that this practice can boost morale, reduce turnover, and enhance productivity.

Knowing when and what to give as a gift can be a significant challenge. Some individuals give gifts to their clients too frequently, while others rarely give gifts because they don't know what to get. The following advice will help you select an appropriate gift for any business occasion while still adhering to the rules of gift-giving.

Stay Practical: The gift you offer should be both practical and meaningful, so it's important to do your research before making a purchase. For instance, if your customer has children, a cute teddy bear could be a thoughtful option to consider, especially if they are traveling with their family on business.

Avoid Holiday Themes: Another guideline for business gift-giving etiquette is to steer clear of seasonal themes. While some companies may go all out with holiday-themed gifts, it's best to avoid this approach. Your gifts should never make customers feel obligated to you, and you should never give the impression that you expect something in return. This also means avoiding gifts that feature Christmas trees or other holiday symbols when the recipient may not share the same holiday celebration.

Include Personalization: Adding a personal touch to your gift is always appreciated. If you're giving a gift to a specific client, consider personalizing it by including their name or any other detail that makes them feel valued. People appreciate the effort you put into making the gift more personalized, such as including a handwritten letter. If the idea of writing individual letters to numerous people for the holidays seems overwhelming, you can consider purchasing gift cards instead.

Learn About Regional Practices: Before giving a gift to a customer from a different country, it's important to familiarize yourself with the business gift-giving customs of their culture. It's better to err on the side of caution than to risk offending someone by offering a gift that may be considered inappropriate or insulting in their cultural context.

It is considered impolite to present a gift during a meal in France. In Japanese culture, it is considered rude to give someone a present until you have established a rapport with them and can gauge their preferences. It is crucial to familiarize yourself with the correct protocol before opening your gift.

Many businesses have policies that prohibit giving gifts to employees, clients, and other business associates due to the complexity of the situation. To avoid awkwardness, it is important to understand the proper protocol for presenting gifts in a professional setting. The ability to give and receive gifts is an integral part of a successful company.

When selecting professional presents, options like food, wine, small conveniences (such as a business-card holder or a pen), and office goods are appropriate choices (e.g., a picture frame or computer accessory). Take care to adhere to your company's gift policy while making your selection. Putting time and effort into choosing the right gift can make the process less daunting.

When offering a gift to a business associate, ensure it is not too personal. Exercise caution when giving funny presents, as it's best to avoid them unless you are certain the recipient will find them humorous.

Excessive extravagance in gift-giving is not only tacky but also offensive. Others may not appreciate your inclination for extravagant gifts and may feel embarrassed or even resentful as a result.

In the business world, gifts of money or tangible items are not always the best way to show appreciation. Volunteering your time or providing assistance to a coworker's or client's workplace charity may be more meaningful and appreciated than a physical gift.

The Ultimate Guide to Professional Gifting Etiquette

"I can't accept that."

That's not exactly what you want to hear when you give a gift to a client or potential client in an effort to show your appreciation.

Company ethics and transparency have always been important, but in recent years, businesses have become stricter in their gift practices, both in giving and receiving business presents. This trend is particularly noticeable in industries such as pharmaceuticals, media, banking and insurance, government, technology, and nonprofits.

Corporate gift-giving policies have become more prevalent as the business world's focus on ethics has led to the adoption of rules regarding gift distribution. This concept is often referred to as "gifts and entertainment policy."

Let's explore the reasons behind these gift-giving guidelines.

Simply put, these regulations exist to ensure that businesses comply with anti-bribery laws. By adhering to these rules, companies can avoid financial troubles, safeguard their professional reputation, and stay out of legal trouble.

The act of giving a gift should ideally be a gesture of gratitude and goodwill. In the past, salespeople and suppliers in thriving industries would often treat customers, who were responsible for significant purchases, to extravagant events and lavish gifts.

In many modern professions, there are now rules that govern who can give and receive gifts, the maximum value of these gifts, and other parameters. These regulations not only discourage corrupt practices but also prevent favoritism and potential conflicts of interest (or the perception of such).

It is crucial for companies that incorporate giveaways into their marketing and sales strategies to be aware of these restrictions. By doing so, they can ensure that their gift-giving practices align with ethical standards and legal requirements.

How Would You Define a Bribe?

As mentioned previously, the General Federal Bribery Statute (18 USCS prec 201(b)) prohibits the corrupt giving, offering, or promising of anything of value to any public official or person selected to be a public official with the intention to influence an official act or to induce the recipient to commit or assist in committing fraud or any other unlawful act.

It's important to note that this legislation applies to all public servants, not just elected politicians. Anyone who testifies in a judicial, legislative, executive, or judicially authorized process is considered a witness and falls under the same provisions.

For businesses seeking to expand internationally, it is essential to familiarize themselves with both the U.S. Anti-Bribery Act and the Foreign

Corrupt Practices Act. These laws, similar to other anti-bribery laws in the United States, make it illegal for businesses and individuals to bribe foreign government officials in order to secure or maintain contracts. This includes offering gifts or other items of value that cannot be purchased with money.

Furthermore, it's important to understand that state and local authorities are subject to anti-bribery statutes in most states. It is necessary to be aware of any gift-giving regulations in your own state or in any state where you intend to conduct business, even if the wording of the laws is similar to federal legislation.

A company must adhere to gift-giving legislation, including anti-bribery statutes, as well as other industry-specific requirements.

In the financial sector, strict guidelines established by the S.E.C. dictate the permissible forms of compensation. These guidelines were initially established in 1940 and have since undergone refinement and revision.

Different statutes govern gifts to public servants, with certain items such as meals, plaques, and other similar presents being excluded.

While gift-giving practices may vary among companies, there are some universal norms that can be expected in their gift policies, especially when considering doing business with them. These may include:

- Specifics about which individuals within the company employees are allowed to give gifts to and the appropriate occasions for doing so.
- Information regarding who from external sources may or may not send gifts to company personnel, as well as the appropriate timing for such gifts.
- Gift-giving guidelines for colleagues, managers, subordinates, and clients.

It is the responsibility of the gift recipient to familiarize themselves with the laws and corporate regulations pertaining to gift acceptance and disclosure. If there is any uncertainty, it is advisable to consult with an accountant or corporate attorney. Since gift policies can vary from one company to another, it is recommended to check with the HR or finance department to obtain any specific guidelines that need to be followed.

It is also important for the gift policy to explicitly state whether manager approval is required for gifts.

Companies often designate the following as no-gift zones in their employee handbooks:

- Individuals in positions of authority
- Gifts that are expensive or extravagant
- Items that come in multiple quantities
- Any recipients for whom the gift may be perceived as a bribe (as defined above), with the intention of influencing a commercial or governmental decision or action (or lack thereof)

Most of the above guidelines also apply to the act of accepting a gift.

Furthermore, employees are prohibited from soliciting gifts or charitable contributions under the company's gift policy. Therefore, it is important for anyone including a handwritten letter with a gift (even if of nominal value) to take precautions to avoid any appearance of bribery.

It is always advisable to err on the side of caution and modesty. In some institutions, a $25 gift may be the maximum allowed. Gift policies are an essential component of the codes of conduct in most major corporations and are designed with clarity and specificity.

Consider items that can be shared among a group, such as cookies, cupcakes, or a team meal. This approach allows the joy of the gift to be spread to an entire team and increases awareness of your business among a broader audience beyond just the main point of contact.

Opt for discreet, unique, and inexpensive gifts. Gift certificates for coffee shops are a safe option, as well as novelty items like personalized socks. These items possess a special touch and can pleasantly surprise recipients. Remember, the goal is for the recipient to think, "That sales agent (or business) is creative, generous, and thoughtful," rather than "Oh no... another trinket that I'll give to my kids" or "This company is clearly trying to 'buy' my purchasing decision."

Gifting an experience, such as admission to a live or online event, along with a token of appreciation and presence, can leave a lasting impression on a client or potential customer. However, it is important to do your research, as this area may still be unclear for many businesses, especially if the cost of the tickets exceeds the company's gift policy.

If you are unsure about anything, don't hesitate to ask! If a customer or potential client declines your gift, take it as an opportunity to explain your company's gift-giving guidelines. Make amends by assuring the recipient that you will respect their policies in the future.

Here are some additional tips on gift-giving and alternative options:

- All-department presents, edible snacks, and inexpensive items with practicality and perceived value are safe choices.
- Show your gift recipients how much you care by being prepared to disclose the gifts you have given. In many organizations, employees are expected to publicly disclose the presents they have received.

Did you know that many businesses have policies against employee gift-giving? The level of awareness surrounding this issue may surprise you, as it is heavily influenced by the company's culture.

Before engaging in gift-giving, familiarize yourself with the company's gift-giving policy. If you have any questions, reach out to someone in the Human Resources department. This will help ensure that things remain comfortable and compliant.

One of the key principles in establishing a gift-giving policy is fairness to everyone. It is uncommon for regulations to impose limits based on the monetary value of gifts or the recipient's position within the organization. For example, an employee giving an expensive gift to a manager may be perceived as trying to gain favor, and a boss giving a gift to one employee over another may be seen as favoritism.

Sometimes, it can be tempting to take a one-size-fits-all approach to gift-giving. However, when it comes to specific occasions such as weddings, career achievements, funerals, and baby showers, it becomes more challenging because not everyone will have the same experiences.

It's also important to consider donating "across" rather than "up" the organizational ladder. This is because some companies have policies against giving presents to individuals in positions of authority. When selecting gifts for managers, whether it's for the holidays or special occasions according to company tradition, apply the same approach as you would for any other recipient.

When working with partners from different parts of the world, it's crucial to respect their cultural norms. Before sending a gift to another country, take the time to learn about their customs, including festivals, gift-giving practices, color symbolism, and even numerical preferences. For example, in China, the color red is associated with good fortune, while the color white is associated with the afterlife and mourning.

Certain gifts may be more appropriate to present outside of the office, or in some cases, not at all. Again, this will depend on the established norms and values of your company. Remember that the act of giving presents should always be done with genuine goodwill and appreciation.

We should exclude gag gifts as a potential option. While a good chuckle is enjoyable, it shouldn't come at the expense of making someone else feel bad. It's important to avoid jokes that target people's age, mental health, physical appearance, disabilities, race, gender, or cultural norms.

When giving a personal gift, it's important not to go overboard with ostentation. While it's understandable to want to choose a gift that the recipient will appreciate, it's best to avoid items that directly relate to their physical appearance, such as lingerie, perfume, or expensive jewelry. Cash should also be avoided as a gift, as it can be interpreted in various ways. Instead, consider giving a digital gift or something more thoughtful and meaningful.

A general rule of thumb is to treat everyone equally and avoid discrimination or sexism in gift-giving. This principle applies both within and outside the company, including when shopping for presents for vendors, customers, and suppliers. It's important to create an inclusive and fair environment for everyone involved.

One strategy is to offer the same type of gift to everyone on the team. If you receive baby shower gifts, for example, consider passing them along to the next coworker who experiences the joy of a new arrival. Collaborative gift-giving is another option, which promotes a sense of teamwork where others can contribute as they see fit. However, it's crucial to ensure that no one on the team feels obligated to make a contribution, and leaders should be understanding that not everyone can or wants to participate. The goal is to provide each employee and occasion with a gift of similar value.

CHAPTER 5

The Importance of Personalization

What Are Personalized Gifts?

Personalized presents are experiencing a significant resurgence. Put simply, a customized gift is an item that incorporates one or more distinguishing marks or characteristics specific to the recipient. This is often achieved by engraving or embossing a person's initials onto a merchandise item.

Several factors contribute to the growing demand for personalized gifts. Businesses are embracing this trend because they recognize that ensuring customer satisfaction is a vital component of their branding, marketing strategy, and problem-solving processes. Furthermore, the extensive range of customizable presents allows for catering to various interests and age groups. In other words, whether the recipient is a pet lover, a sports enthusiast, a food connoisseur, a technology aficionado, or any other type of person, there is likely a suitable personalized gift available.

For a gift to be considered truly "personalized," it should include the recipient's full name, encompassing both the given name and surname, along with their initials. The ability to incorporate artwork, images, and corporate logos into personalized gifts has expanded in recent years. These gifts can be crafted in a variety of styles, color schemes, and techniques, catering to the individual preferences of the recipient.

Companies carefully monitor how customers perceive and respond to personalized offerings. Continuous product innovation is crucial for a successful company strategy in today's market, as businesses need to adapt to evolving customer demands to maximize profitability.

The global market for personalized gifts is flourishing due to the increased accessibility of the internet and the growing production of customized items worldwide.

One of the key driving factors behind the global demand for customized gifts is the rising frequency of gift exchanges to commemorate various occasions. Technological advancements have facilitated the development of new and improved products that appeal to a wide audience.

At times, personalized gifts can tell a lifelong story. They have the power to evoke cherished memories and express deep affection. For instance, consider a picture gift that can be customized with the recipient's favorite image. By printing it on a product and presenting it to them or their parents, you can witness their joy and gratitude firsthand.

This goes beyond a simple thank-you or token of gratitude. When you gift someone with a cherished item, it holds far more meaning than a mere gesture of appreciation. It becomes a symbol of the unique connection you share, demonstrating that you value them as individuals and appreciate their distinctiveness. This is not just an ordinary store-bought teddy bear. Personalized presents, in a deeply personal way, are the ultimate form of gift-giving. They signify the beginning of a connection, honor its existence, and strengthen it over time. This is the pinnacle of activities that foster group unity.

Indeed, when you give someone a unique present, you convey a multitude of messages. First, you express your confidence in your understanding of the recipient by selecting a gift that you know they will truly enjoy. Let's say hockey is their passion. A hockey stick with their name on it would make a fantastic gift. Additionally, by taking the time to personalize a gift, you demonstrate that you care enough to consider their interests and preferences, and that you want to give them something truly special. You can be certain that they will love it.

Personalizing a gift allows you to showcase the thought and care you have put into it, while also providing a wonderful opportunity to express your affection for the recipient. This is the power of a personalized present: it enables you to focus on the connection, shower it with praise, and solidify the bond between you and the recipient over time.

As individuals, we prefer to believe that we stand out from the crowd, and the same holds true for the people we care about. That's why the greatest personalized presents take into account every peculiarity, taste, and characteristic of the recipient.

The finest gifts are those crafted with thoughtfulness and reflect the recipient. They are the type of presents that everyone would cherish receiving.

Therefore, presenting a customized gift is the ultimate way to convey sincerity and love. It goes beyond personal preferences; it is about the recipient and what they genuinely appreciate.

Gift-giving serves as a means for people to open up and share their deepest desires and heartfelt greetings with one another, which is why this practice is widely embraced and celebrated during festive occasions. Since the dawn of human existence, exchanging gifts has been a cherished tradition. Being on the receiving end of a remarkable gift is always special, especially if it also provides the giver with a memorable and fulfilling experience. Thus, the true aesthetic value of a gift resides in the emotions it evokes. The battle of gift-giving is won when the recipient experiences feelings of joy, happiness, and love due to the heartfelt gesture. Personalized presents bring a unique touch to the act of giving, thanks to their one-of-a-kind nature and creativity.

Even the most generic celebration can be transformed into something special by presenting a thoughtfully personalized and unique gift. Adding a name, a photo, or a heartfelt note to a gift is a kind way for individuals to express their appreciation for those they care about.

The Benefits of Personalized Gifts

If you want to demonstrate the value you place on your connection with someone, a thoughtful and personalized gift is the ideal choice. It signifies that you have taken the extra effort to select a present that holds meaning. Let's delve deeper into the merits of personalized gifts.

Personalized presents provide a wonderful way to express your emotions, ideas, and memories about the recipient. "Personalization" refers to the practice of adding a special touch to a gift through carefully chosen words, a specific theme, or a completely unique design. While the gift itself may fade from memory, the words will remain etched in the recipient's mind and heart. The words you select to convey your message need not be poetic, but they should hold significance for both of you.

When you invest time and effort into customizing a gift, you can ensure that it stands out as one-of-a-kind. For example, if you have a personalized message engraved on a watch or ring, it becomes a truly unique piece. Incorporating a personal touch that reflects the special nature of your connection elevates the gift's meaning and enhances its appreciation. Thoughtful touches that demonstrate your care for the recipient will make your presents truly special and memorable.

Regardless of the holiday or occasion, a personalized gift is always well-received. Whether it's a housewarming, a birthday, a retirement, or an upcoming vacation, a thoughtful and customized present is always welcome. It's easy to add your own special touch to any item or gift; just keep the occasion in mind while creating it. For instance, if you purchase a golden picture frame for someone's birthday, you can repurpose it as a retirement gift by swapping out the photo, engraving, and packaging accordingly.

Gifts specifically tailored for the recipient are universally appreciated, regardless of age. Whether it's a beautiful necklace for a birthday, engraved cufflinks for a groom, or a cuddly teddy bear for a newborn, these thoughtful gifts are cherished because they show that the recipient was carefully considered during the gift selection process. People from all walks of life appreciate gestures that demonstrate thoughtful consideration.

Research plays a vital role in the customization process. Taking the time to learn more about the recipient's preferences and interests allows you to tailor the gift accordingly. If you don't have all the necessary information about the recipient, you can always seek assistance from those close to them.

Adding a personal touch, such as incorporating the recipient's own artistic or graphic style, or including a meaningful item, transforms a generic gift into something truly special. Personalizing a gift with a name, an image, or a brief note is a heartfelt way to express to loved ones how much they mean to you.

The adage that the thought behind a gift is more important than the gift itself holds true, particularly when it comes to personalized presents. There are numerous methods to personalize a gift, depending on the item and materials used, which showcase the time and consideration put into its selection. For instance, when gifting jewelry, you could have the recipient's name or a meaningful symbol engraved on the piece. Alternatively, you could purchase a phone cover featuring a picture or quote that you know they will appreciate.

The ultimate goal is to provide the recipient with an item that will be cherished and kept for a long time. While flowers and chocolates may lose their luster, a well-crafted keepsake can be treasured for years to come. Every time the recipient uses or sees your thoughtful gift, it will evoke fond memories of the good times you shared together.

Moreover, a personalized gift showcases the extra thought and effort you've put into ensuring it aligns with the recipient's desires and appreciation. Customized presents hold significant meaning for partners as they demonstrate the giver's affection and gratitude for the receiver. Whether you're shopping for him or her, a personalized gift is a thoughtful and distinctive way to convey your emotions.

Let's face it: shopping for someone who is not your age or gender, especially if you don't know them well, can be quite challenging. Similarly, it can be difficult to select an appropriate gift for someone you know very well. However, personalized gifts can make this task easier. Regardless of your level of familiarity with the recipient or their age, you can find a thoughtful and unique gift that they will cherish. By choosing an item that holds personal significance for them, such as incorporating their name, date of birth, favorite symbol or color, images, or a meaningful message, you can ensure you have selected the perfect gift.

There is no greater joy than witnessing someone genuinely appreciate the gift you've given them. However, that joy can quickly turn to disappointment if you discover they already have something similar. By offering a truly special and personalized gift, you can avoid this situation. Including their name or a picture of them in the presentation ensures your gift will be one-of-a-kind and leave a lasting impression.

Personalized gifts serve as a heartfelt token of affection. They contribute to the growth of connections that endure throughout one's lifetime. When an individual receives a well-crafted personalized gift, they feel loved and valued for their unique place in the giver's life.

Personalized gifts adorned with priceless photographs of special occasions or events allow recipients to dive into the sea of nostalgia and reminisce about their happiest moments. It's more than just a gift; the personalized item evokes warm feelings every time your loved one uses it.

Almost every occasion calls for a unique and personalized gift rather than a generic one. Whether it's your child's first birthday, your parents' golden wedding anniversary, a religious holiday, or a celebration of your own success, you can always come up with a thoughtful gift. Adding a personalized touch to a little birthday bash or presenting a joyful photo for a couple's wedding anniversary adds a touch of magic to every celebration. Similarly, if you want to wow your sweetheart on Valentine's Day or surprise your grandparents with a heartfelt gift on Grandparents Day, a personalized gift is always appreciated, regardless of the recipient's age or the nature of the relationship.

Surprising your coworkers and clients with items that are in tune with the latest trends and popular culture can be a great way to show you care. Here are a few popular items right now:

1. **Wireless Earbuds**: Brands like Apple AirPods and Samsung Galaxy Buds are very popular. They make listening to music, taking calls, and watching videos convenient and wire-free.

2. **Fitness Trackers**: Devices like the Fitbit or Apple Watch are trendy for those interested in health and wellness. They help track steps, monitor heart rate, and even analyze sleep patterns.

3. **Graphic T-Shirts**: T-shirts featuring popular TV shows, movies, or funny sayings are always a hit. They are a fun, casual way to show off what you love.

4. **Instant Cameras**: Brands like Fujifilm Instax have become popular again, especially for younger crowds. They offer a fun way to capture moments and instantly have a physical photo.

These gifts tap into current trends and can bring a smile to your loved ones' faces by showing that you know what they enjoy.

Personalized gifts are perfect for milestone occasions such as birthdays, anniversaries, and farewells when words alone can't express how much someone means to us. They become a heartfelt expression of sentiments and cherished memories. Personalized gifts elevate ordinary presents to the realm of true rarity.

While we have mainly focused on the benefits for the gift recipients so far, personalized gifts also offer advantages for the companies themselves. Many businesses provide their employees with swag bags containing branded pens, notebooks, books, or t-shirts. These gestures are highly appreciated by the employees and also help promote the company's positive image.

Employees play a crucial role in the functioning of any company. They handle routine tasks such as answering phones and managing databases, as well as more complex and skill-based responsibilities like building customer relationships and evaluating market trends. When employees feel appreciated, they become more engaged with the company as a whole, resulting in increased productivity and stronger loyalty towards their employer.

Verbal appreciation is one way to show your gratitude to your staff, and presenting them with a unique and carefully chosen gift is another effective method. The choice of the perfect gift depends on factors such as the company's budget, the employee's contribution, and their personal preferences. To select an appropriate gift for an employee, it is crucial to have knowledge of the available options and understand the recipient's individual tastes.

Sometimes, the simplest things hold the most significance. Do you know what the employee enjoys or have they mentioned needing something practical, like a calendar, paperweight, or office supplies? It is important to choose a gift that the recipient will actually use or proudly display. Giving a gift that has little utility or value would be a waste of money.

While socks, video games, and shiny new appliances are suitable for close friends and family, they may not be the best choices for employees. Workplace decorations and gadgets such as clocks, cacti, mouse pads, phone stands, and engraved plaques are more appropriate gifts for employees. Additionally, consider items that employees can take with them, such as reusable shopping bags, keychains, company-branded clothing, and drinkware, as they are not only practical but also highly appreciated.

As a general guideline, it is advisable to keep the gift options straightforward. Choosing gifts that have broad appeal across different ages and backgrounds is a safe and reliable option.

Giving unexpected and thoughtful gifts to colleagues has multiple advantages. It can boost morale, foster teamwork, and increase job satisfaction by recognizing and rewarding individuals for their contributions. Employee burnout is a common issue in the workplace, and it's important to support staff in dealing with stress and feeling overwhelmed.

Encourage open communication and create an environment where employees feel comfortable expressing their feelings. Understanding their concerns and sources of stress allows you to provide better assistance. Is there a specific challenge they are facing? Are there difficult clients or tasks causing stress?

Physical, personalized gifts have a stronger impact than mere words of praise in keeping employees engaged and invested in their work. They convey that you recognize and appreciate their efforts, initiative, and creativity. Even small gestures can significantly uplift the spirits of employees who may be feeling down due to workload, recent criticism, or other factors.

There are various reasons to celebrate with a party, such as an employee's milestone anniversary with the company, the successful completion of a challenging project, or the announcement of a promotion. Consider giving employees engraved plaques, trophies, or other rewards to recognize their achievements.

Acknowledging accomplishments outside of the workplace is also important. Individual milestones, such as birthdays, weddings, or the arrival of a new baby, should be celebrated with a company-wide event, particularly if you have a smaller staff. This presents an excellent opportunity to demonstrate that you care about your employees as individuals beyond their professional roles.

Personalizing gifts for employees has additional positive effects, such as fostering closer relationships among colleagues. It's important to recognize that people who work for you, especially those who are less experienced or easily intimidated, may perceive you as intimidating due to your position in the company hierarchy.

Whether it's personalized candles, tote bags, mugs, or any other item, expressing appreciation for your staff through customized gifts shows that you not only see who they are but also pay attention to their individual preferences and interests. This not only helps build rapport with your employees but also establishes trust in your leadership.

By fostering stronger relationships among employees, you can create a sense of community in the workplace, making it feel less like just another location to fulfill working hours. Work doesn't have to be dull simply because it's done every day. Small and thoughtful gestures can have a significant impact.

On important work holidays and celebratory occasions like birthdays, demonstrating appreciation by organizing parties, providing lunch, and giving customized gifts can greatly contribute to being seen as an employer of choice. These exciting events offer a pleasant break from the monotony of the workday, allowing employees to set aside their daily tasks momentarily and enjoy some fun.

When you show genuine appreciation for your employees' efforts and provide them with meaningful rewards, you create an atmosphere where people genuinely want to come to work. A content workforce is more likely to be dedicated to the company's success and have a positive outlook on its future prospects. Giving personalized gifts is an excellent way to show your employees that you value their hard work and dedication.

The Importance of Personalization: A Real-World Case Study in Creating Lasting Impressions

In the world of business, creating lasting impressions can be the key to nurturing client relationships and attracting new prospects. Strategic corporate gifting is a powerful tool for achieving this goal. Let's explore a real-world example that demonstrates how these principles can be put into action with remarkable results.

On February 2nd, 2022 (2/2/22), an event called "2's Day with Shay" took place in Orlando, Florida, featuring Shay Rowbottom, a prominent figure in LinkedIn marketing and personal branding. This event presented a perfect opportunity to showcase the power of thoughtful corporate gifting. Recognizing this potential, we approached Foureva Media, the agency representing Shay, with a proposal to sponsor the event through personalized corporate gifts for attendees.

Our approach to this event encompassed several key strategies. First and foremost, we carefully considered the choice of gift. We selected branded candles, a decision that aligned perfectly with our gifting principles. These candles were not only practical items that attendees would likely use, but with over 100 hours of burn time, they also ensured a lasting reminder of the event and Shay's brand. This longevity is crucial in creating an enduring impression, as it extends the positive associations from the event long after it has concluded.

Personalization played a vital role in our gifting strategy. Each candle featured a custom label, tailored to reflect Shay's brand and the unique "2's Day" theme of the event. This attention to detail demonstrated thoughtfulness and enhanced the perceived value of the gift, making recipients feel truly special.

One of the most impactful aspects of our strategy was the differentiated approach we took for current and potential clients. Current clients received the branded candles as a token of appreciation, reinforcing their loyalty and the value placed on their ongoing relationship. Potential clients, on the other hand, were given an "extra" gift. This additional gesture created a positive first impression and provided an incentive for further engagement with Shay's services. By tailoring our approach to different audience segments, we maximized the impact of our gifting strategy.

The execution of our gifting plan was carefully considered to enhance its effectiveness. We set up a strategically placed booth near the exit, ensuring every attendee would pass by as they left the event. This positioning allowed us to capture attendees when they were in high spirits, provide a final positive interaction associated with Shay's brand, and differentiate between current and potential clients as we offered the appropriate gift to each.

The results of this strategic gifting approach were immediately apparent. We observed genuine smiles and expressions of surprise from both current and potential clients as they received their gifts. Many recipients paused to examine the candles, often commenting on the personalized labels and the thoughtfulness behind the gift. This engagement created natural opportunities for brief, friendly interactions, allowing for last-minute connections and reinforcing the positive experience of the event.

Perhaps most importantly, as attendees left with their branded candles, they carried a physical reminder of Shay's brand and the event. This tangible takeaway extends the impact of the event beyond the day itself, creating a lasting impression that can influence future business decisions.

The differentiated approach for potential clients proved particularly effective. Those who received the "extra" gift often expressed additional appreciation, potentially setting a positive foundation for future business relationships. This demonstrates how strategic gifting can be a powerful tool in nurturing new business opportunities.

Several key takeaways emerged from this experience:

1. Strategic timing is crucial. By distributing gifts at the end of the event, we ensured that the positive experience of receiving a gift was the last impression attendees had.

2. Alignment with brand and event themes creates a cohesive experience. The personalized candles complemented both the "2's Day" theme and Shay's brand, enhancing the overall impact.

3. A differentiated approach allows for simultaneous nurturing of existing relationships and attraction of new ones. By offering slightly different gifts to current and potential clients, we were able to cater to the specific needs of each group.

4. The longevity of the gift plays a significant role in creating lasting impressions. Choosing a gift with extended usability (100+ hours of burn time) ensured that the positive associations from the event would be reinforced over time.

5. The immediate reactions – smiles, engagement, and positive comments – provided tangible validation of the gifting strategy's effectiveness.

This real-world example demonstrates how strategic corporate gifting principles can be applied to create lasting impressions that extend well beyond a single event. By carefully selecting gifts, personalizing them, and strategically distributing them, we were able to strengthen relationships with current clients while also laying the groundwork for potential new business opportunities.

In today's competitive business landscape, these lasting impressions can be the difference between a one-time interaction and a long-term, mutually beneficial relationship. As you apply these strategies in your own corporate gifting efforts, remember that each gift is an opportunity to create a positive, lasting connection with your clients and prospects.

Reasons Why Personalized Gifts Are the Best

Without a doubt, personalized gifts have become a significant trend in the gift-giving industry. What could be better than a gift that can be transformed into something truly personal with the simple addition of a name or a heartfelt message? After all, the purpose of giving a gift is to convey your emotions through the gesture, so incorporating your thoughts into the gift from the start makes perfect sense.

The tradition of giving gifts is a thoughtful way to express goodwill and heartfelt sentiments on special occasions, and it dates back as far as civilization itself. Receiving a fantastic gift is a wonderful experience in itself, and it also provides the giver with a sense of fulfillment that lasts long. When gifts are as unique and creative as those that can be ordered online, the act of giving them becomes even more exceptional.

However, gift-giving is not always easy. Finding a one-of-a-kind gift for a friend, partner, or family member can be challenging. It's tempting to quickly browse through strip malls or online stores, but that can make the process mundane. Giving gifts should be an enjoyable experience, an opportunity to pleasantly surprise someone and offer them a gift they will cherish forever.

Fortunately, the rise of online retailers has made it easier to employ creative gift-giving strategies. With a wide array of products available, each vying to be the "perfect gift," it's not difficult to choose a last-minute gift for someone. But does that make it unique and personal? I don't think so, and here's why. It lacks the individual touch.

There is no denying that personalized gifts have evolved into a thriving industry of their own. What could be better than a unique gift for someone special that becomes even more memorable with the addition of their name or a heartfelt message? Considering that gift-giving is intrinsically tied to conveying emotions through material means, it only makes sense to infuse your heartfelt wishes into the gift right from the start.

CHAPTER 6

Use Corporate Gifting for Business Growth

Building strong business ties is indeed a valuable pursuit, but it can be challenging to do so in a purposeful and systematic manner that yields a return on investment. To optimize your corporate giving program for maximum impact and identify which partnerships to cultivate, let's delve into leveraging giving as a strategic business development strategy.

Developing commercial partnerships not only fosters growth but also generates brand advocates. Brand evangelists are individuals who have unwavering faith in your product or service and actively recommend it to others. This level of advocacy extends beyond a positive experience; it stems from their emotional attachment to your company. Brand evangelists naturally favor your brand over competitors, often without even realizing it. Their belief in your company's worth drives them to promote it to others, resulting in organic brand recognition growth and increased mindshare.

Gifting is one effective method to create brand enthusiasts. Thoughtfully selecting a gift and delivering it promptly, accompanied by a sincere letter, demonstrates your respect and admiration for the recipient. The act of giving establishes a connection and fosters a relationship on an emotional level.

It is widely known that people who have a positive connection with someone are willing to go the extra mile for them. This can lead to increased recommendations for your company, ultimately boosting sales and generating revenue.

By strategically incorporating gifting into your business development strategy, you can cultivate brand advocates who will actively support and promote your brand. This not only strengthens your business ties but also drives growth and enhances your overall success.

With Whom Should You Establish Connections

Clients are the obvious answer for the majority of businesses. Gaining new customers and maintaining existing ones are both necessary for company growth.

However, there are a lot of other individuals that support your company's success, and they too should be recognized.

Employees: Your employees are crucial for good public relations. If they have a positive relationship with your company, they will naturally promote it by talking about how great it is to work there, sharing the company's positive actions and social media posts with others. This helps spread good words about your company far and wide. Employees can become brand advocates, supporting your company's culture and boosting its image, which is highly beneficial.

The necessity of staff retention is also crucial. Businesses lose money and opportunities due to employee turnover, but workers who feel valued are more inclined to stick around.

Partners: Partners are crucial to the success of your company. Think of them as the gears that keep the machine running smoothly. For example, a small construction firm relies heavily on skilled contractors like electricians and plumbers to complete various projects. These individuals are not on the company's payroll but their expertise and timely work contribute significantly to the project's success. Recognizing and appreciating these contributors ensures they feel valued and are likely to speak well of your company to others. When a potential client inquires, these partners are more inclined to share positive experiences, thus enhancing your company's reputation.

Vendors: Vendors can significantly impact your company's bottom line and lead generation efforts by helping you better serve your customers. Maintaining a positive relationship of gratitude with your suppliers can pave the way for collaboration and assistance during challenging times. They are not only a source of goods and services but also potential clients, contacts, and networking opportunities. Including a small token of appreciation in your budget can show your new connections how much they mean to you.

Partners for Referral: Similarly, referrals from trusted partners can be a goldmine for new business opportunities. Consider a real estate agency that works closely with local moving companies. When someone buys a new home, the real estate agent can recommend a trusted mover. If the movers feel appreciated and have a good relationship with the real-tors, they're more likely to return the favor by suggesting their clients to that particular real estate agency first. By nurturing these relationships, expressing genuine gratitude, and maintaining regular communication, you ensure your business stays at the top of the referral list, opening doors to new customers who trust the recommendations of their current service providers.

How Do You Choose the Ideal Occasion?

This is a question that often puzzles marketers and gifting teams. Even though Christmas is the most popular occasion for receiving presents, it may not always be the most memorable. Take a moment to consider it: There's a lot of hustle and bustle during that time of year, and many people are reuniting with long-lost family members. As a result, your gift can easily get lost in the noise, as there is already a lot happening.

Looking back at some of the most successful gift programs we've created for corporate customers, we can see that many of them capitalized on unexpected timing to have the greatest impact on their recipients. For example:

- Giving presents to commemorate a business achievement.
- Offering gifts to congratulate new hires or commemorate staff anniversaries.
- Sharing gifts to support public relations or gain social media publicity.
- Providing rewards to partners and colleagues after completing a project.

By sending gifts during any of these occasions, you invite your recipients to celebrate with you, which can help strengthen your relationship.

Which Message Delivers the Biggest Impact?

Selecting the right gift for business relationships can be tough, especially when you're sending them to many people in different places. Even if you're buying lots of gifts at once, there are still ways to make each one feel special and tailored to the recipient.

For instance, if you know that some of your clients live in colder areas, you might choose to send them high-quality scarves or gloves. On the other hand, for those in warmer climates, a set of quality sunglasses or a branded sun hat could be a better choice. This shows that you're paying attention to their specific needs based on where they live.

Another way to personalize gifts in bulk is by choosing items that can be customized with the recipient's name or initials. Things like personalized notebooks or water bottles add a personal touch that can make the recipients feel valued and appreciated.

Corporate giving is not a new concept, but it has significantly evolved since the pandemic. According to a recent survey, 35% of respondents mentioned that they have given more gifts than usual since transitioning to remote work. Of those who increased their gift-giving frequency, nearly 60% did so to maintain relationships with their customers, while approximately 66% did it to keep their staff engaged and motivated.

One Thing is Crystal Clear: Corporate Gifts Bring Benefits to Businesses

Here are some compelling reasons to consider giving business gifts to potential customers, clients, and employees.

First, attract potential customers. By offering a thoughtful and personalized gift to a potential consumer, you can gain an advantage over the competition. This approach helps you steer clear of generic sales pitches that often end up in the spam folder, making your next message truly stand out.

And let's be honest, who doesn't enjoy opening a gift? It creates a positive and memorable experience for the recipient, leaving a lasting impression.

The Second Objective is to Convert Prospects Into Paying Customers

Building connections is vital for the success of any business. That's why initiating discussions with a small gift can lead to almost double the revenue compared to not doing so. It's as simple as leaving a lasting impression with thoughtful business gifts. An original and meaningful gift is 2.3 times more likely to prompt the desired behavior, such as converting a lead into a customer.

A compelling example of how meaningful gifts can significantly increase customer conversions involves the company Obvi. They conducted an A/B test where they offered a free gift with the second order of their subscription service [6]. This strategic gift significantly increased their conversion rates—customers who knew they would receive a free gift with their second order were 85% more likely to follow through with their purchase compared to those who weren't offered a gift. This test not only boosted their immediate conversions but also helped Obvi in reducing cancellations and order skips, underlining the impact of thoughtful gifting on customer retention and business growth

Here's more evidence that corporate gifts are valuable when it comes to persuasion without being pushy: Non-customers can be enticed to become customers through the power of gifts. In fact, 80% of customers feel more inclined to engage with a company that provides personalized experiences. The right gift, sent at the right time, can motivate potential customers to take the next step in the sales process, whether that's making a purchase, signing up for a service, or scheduling a discovery call.

Third, to Always Keep Your Company Top-of-mind

Carefully curated gift baskets by experts are an excellent way to maintain the interest of long-term clients and prospects who may be slow to convert. Alternatively, a custom candle with a thoughtful touch can also achieve the same effect!

When clients or customers remember a company gift, it results in a 40% increase in return on investment. With extensive data supporting this notion, there is little room for debate.

Next, to Make Customers Feel Valued

Every customer, especially those who have previously supported your business, should be treated with respect and appreciation. You can't simply rely on the money they provide without reciprocating in some way. Think of it as a continuous cycle of give-and-take that needs to be nurtured.

A well-chosen "just because" gift can strengthen the bond between a company and its customers. Research in the retail industry has shown that customers who have an emotional connection with a brand are worth 306% more to the business over their lifetime [7]. Expressing gratitude with even a small gift can have a significant impact.

Another Objective is to Boost Customer Loyalty and Retain Existing Customers

In addition to making your customers feel appreciated, this gesture of kindness may encourage them to continue doing business with you. Personal, thoughtful presents can be a powerful tool in combating customer attrition. And it's not just limited to your customers...

Next, to Energize Your Staff

Acknowledge the efforts of your employees. A high-quality, individually designed present can do wonders for morale and team spirit. The success of this is reflected in how your staff approaches their responsibilities and the quality of service they provide to your company's partners, customers, and leads.

Boosting brand loyalty is another benefit.

You want to raise your company's profile by strengthening your business connections, right? Corporate gifting is one strategy to facilitate this. As a business, your reputation should be a top priority, just as profitability is. To succeed, you must prioritize humanizing your business, establishing a favorable reputation, fostering connections, nurturing goodwill, and boosting brand recognition. This sparks customer devotion and increases revenue.

Although these factors do have an effect on sales, they are not always easy to quantify.

And then, to finally boost sales and generate revenue.

Just how quantifiable is everything? Sales. The return on investment (ROI) from promotions like discounts and targeted mailings may not be as high. However, sending tangible presents can help you build long-lasting relationships with customers and staff, which in turn can boost your business's bottom line. So, in this manner, everything works out well for everyone.

When your ads invade your clients' personal space, you've finally achieved advertising's holy grail. When you factor in practicality and client happiness, you're that much closer to the pinnacle of success. Carefully consider what kind of advertising might have such an effect on a consumer.

Simply put, the solution is "corporate giving."

According to a recent BPMA study, after receiving a corporate gift, 56% of respondents reported having a much more favorable impression of the company, and 79% expressed their willingness to do business with the company again [8].

Giving corporate gifts is an effective way to increase brand visibility and establish a presence in the minds of your target audience. Moreover, it allows you to become a part of their daily lives. However, the question remains: How exactly can corporate gifts help promote a company? Let's delve into the ways you can maximize the marketing potential of your promotional items.

One strategy to make the most out of your gift-giving budget is to implement a tiered approach. Not all customers have the same level of importance to your business, and therefore, not all customers should receive the same gift. It's essential to have a promotional gifting strategy with multiple tiers that align with the increasing significance of the customer to your business.

For customers in the third tier, you can consider cost-effective items like calendars that provide value without breaking the bank. For the second tier, opt for slightly more expensive gifts such as T-shirts. Reserve the top-tier gifts, known as "tier one," for your most valuable customers. These gifts should be both useful and beloved, like branded coffee cups. A branded mug with your logo serves as an excellent promotional item as it helps establish your brand in the minds of your audience and continues to do so even after the cup has been received.

By implementing a tiered approach and selecting thoughtful gifts for each tier, you can maximize the impact of your corporate gifts and enhance your brand's visibility and recognition among your target audience.

Make a Plan for Your Advancement

Several factors, such as the recipient's demographics and interests, contribute to the promotional value of a corporate gift. Determine the purpose behind providing gifts. Are you aiming to enhance customer loyalty or generate new leads? Small tokens of appreciation like pens can effectively demonstrate to customers how much you value their business.

Consider providing useful items like umbrellas and tote bags as promotional giveaways. These items can help spread awareness about your business. An attractive customized umbrella in vibrant colors can catch the attention of many people and significantly increase your company's visibility.

Third, Plan Out Your Finances

Instead of viewing promotional items as a mere expense, consider them as an investment. Allocate funds for promotional giveaways on a regular basis, not just during holidays. By consistently providing freebies, you can keep your business in the minds of your clients. Setting a spending limit for corporate gifts can also prevent any adverse impact on your bottom line.

Promotional items are an excellent way to create brand awareness and promote your business. However, it's crucial to approach corporate giving strategically to avoid unnecessary financial strain. Determine the objectives you want to achieve for your company and choose gifts that align with those goals.

Giving corporate gifts offers various benefits, such as building relationships with customers, partners, and stakeholders, boosting morale among your staff, and showcasing your company's ethical standards and commitment to helping others. Effective use of corporate gifts can enhance brand loyalty, generate word-of-mouth publicity, maintain a positive company image, and attract new customers.

Now, Let's Talk About Employees

Employees are the backbone of any business, and receiving presents is always appreciated. Providing them with valuable gifts increases the likelihood of them remembering your business in the future. It can be as simple as giving them a keychain or a branded t-shirt.

Giving gifts to employees within an organization is an excellent way to express appreciation for their efforts and motivate them to continue working hard. Corporate gift giving has been shown to increase employee loyalty and job satisfaction. Distributing company presents at shareholder meetings can also make investors feel valued and appreciated.

When selecting gifts for business associates, opt for items that are durable and useful, ensuring they can be used frequently. Printing your logo and slogan on unique merchandise is a great way to promote brand recognition.

Compared to the cost of financial incentives for employees, clients, and customers, corporate presents are a cost-effective option. Purchasing in bulk can help save money. Thoughtful and well-executed gift-giving programs benefit local businesses, suppliers, and potential partners.

Companies of all types find unique uses for promotional goods and gifts. Explore the possibilities of incorporating promotional items throughout your company by considering the suggestions below. Do you prefer high-end business presents or more functional items? Regardless of your goal, thoughtful and strategic corporate gifting is sure to help you achieve it.

Merchandise is often misunderstood, with the widespread assumption that it must be expensive. To determine the return on investment for promotional products, it's best to sit down and conduct a cost-benefit analysis.

Some Things to Keep in Mind When Looking for the Best Present...

Before embarking on a corporate gift or branded item initiative, it's important to consider several factors. Take the time to carefully think about the recipient and the occasion when choosing a gift. To help guide your decision-making process, let's explore the following questions:

First, identify your target audience. Are they internal or external recipients?

Internal recipients refer to people within your staff, such as employees and team members. They are part of your organization.

External recipients encompass all customers, both past and present, as well as anyone else who interacts with your business but is not an employee. These individuals are external to your organization.

By understanding the distinction between internal and external receivers, you can tailor your gift choices and strategies accordingly to effectively engage and connect with each group.

Secondly, What Kind of People Are They?

When selecting corporate gifts or branded items, it's important to keep in mind various demographic factors such as age, gender, and locality. Additionally, consider the recipient's position within the company or organization.

For practicality and convenience, opt for gifts that are light, compact, and sturdy. This ensures that they won't break easily, especially if they need to be shipped across the nation. It's also crucial to avoid sending items that could melt or spoil if exposed to heat during transit.

By considering these factors, you can choose gifts that align with the recipients' preferences and needs while ensuring the items arrive in good condition, regardless of their location.

Thirdly, What Motivates Them to Do What They Do?

Giving someone a present that demonstrates thoughtful consideration of their interests and hobbies can have a significant impact on your relationship. Take the time to identify the type of gift that would truly resonate with your ideal client or customer, and then create a solution centered around it.

What is the Event?

Is there a specific festival or season associated with the occasion? Is there something to celebrate or commemorate? Alternatively, is it simply a token of appreciation? Considering the context and purpose of the gift will help you choose the most appropriate and meaningful present for the recipient.

What Special Touches Will You Add to the Present?

Corporate gifts that are customized specifically for the recipient are highly appreciated. However, it's important to consider the impact of branding on the perceived value of the gift before making your final decision. Find a way to incorporate your brand in a stylish and prominent manner, ensuring that the design is tasteful and well-executed. By doing so, you can effectively integrate your brand into the gift without diminishing its overall appeal.

How Will You Present the Present?

Having custom packaging for your product can make it truly stand out among competitors. Whether it's customized boxes, bags, or even wrapping paper and ribbon, we can provide you with a wide range of options. Don't limit yourself to traditional packaging; think creatively and find practical uses for the packaging itself. For example, you can use a tote bag or a metal bucket instead of a standard basket for your gift hamper.

It's not uncommon for businesses to overlook employee gifts until the last minute. The complexity of the process often leads to avoidance. However, it's important to remember that planning ahead and buying in bulk can result in significant cost savings. By purchasing gifts in advance and in large quantities, you can streamline the process and ensure that you're prepared without overspending.

What Should You Give as a Corporate Gift? The Golden Question!

These days, you have a wide range of options when it comes to gifting. To create enviable gifts, it's essential to nail the theme and concept. While it's impossible to list all the possibilities, let's explore a few ideas to ignite your creativity!

Alcohol: Spirits, beer, wine, or champagne are popular gifts, but they can sometimes feel impersonal as they have been commonly used. However, if your client is a passionate red wine enthusiast and you've sourced an excellent Shiraz that you know they'll love, it can still be a suitable choice. If the occasion calls for it, consider incorporating the alcohol into a hamper or create branded packaging to add uniqueness and a "wow factor." Leather cases, cloth wraps, or premium carry bags can elevate the presentation.

* A word about alcohol and corporate gifting: Earlier, we mentioned that it's generally a good idea to be cautious when gifting liquor in corporate settings. However, alcohol can still make a great gift if you understand the recipient and gifting etiquette well. Exercise discretion when working with alcohol!

Office items: Everyday stationery items like pens, notepads, and mouse pads are practical and have their place at events. However, they are quite common. If your goal is to differentiate your brand, think outside the box. Consider leather-bound monogrammed journals, iPad holders, or high-quality boxed pens as executive gifts. Aim for the best quality you can afford to make a lasting impression.

Leisure items: This category allows for more creativity, and if chosen wisely, your gifts will be enjoyed repeatedly. The key with leisure items is to apply your brand in a creative way that feels designer. Beach umbrellas, custom flip-flops, beach towels, wine coolers, bar accessories, glassware, cheese boards, and picnic sets can make fantastic gifts, especially when combined together in a themed gift pack. Have fun and aim for items that align with your recipient's interests and lifestyle.

Technology & Tools: Technology and tools are highly sought after in certain industries, but it can be challenging to find high-quality items that your recipients will actually use. In addition to USB drives, companies are now opting for Bluetooth speakers, earbuds, multipurpose chargers, digital frames, and computer accessory kits. Ensure that the technology or tool aligns with your recipient's needs and preferences.

Food items: Food items are a popular choice for corporate gifts as they can be shared with colleagues or enjoyed at home with family. However, they can sometimes come across as generic, so it's important to be creative and thoughtful. Understand your recipient's tastes and preferences before selecting the gift. Creating themed "foodie" experiences can add a fun touch. Consider the container for the gift, which could be a reusable item. Keep in mind that food items may not be suitable if they need to travel or are likely to be exposed to hot or cold conditions that could cause spoilage.

Drinkware: Branded drink bottles and mugs are commonly associated with corporate merchandise and can be executed exceptionally well. There is a wide range of elegant and high-quality options available, including eco-friendly choices, that are worth considering. Bamboo travel coffee mugs, vacuum flasks, coffee mug sets, metal wine coolers, and desktop water jug/cup sets are among the most popular choices in this category.

Health, Home & Personal items: These items can be a good fit for specific industries or may not be appropriate at all, depending on the recipient. Towels, first aid kits, wallets, manicure sets, cufflinks, or mirrors can make excellent gift options. Lifestyle items that can be used around the home are also popular, such as pizza slicers, salt and pepper mills, LED clocks, salad servers, BBQ sets, or folding chairs. Consider the recipient's interests and preferences when selecting from this category.

What's Next?

So now you have gained some insights into the benefits and strategies of using personalized corporate gifts. Now, let's move on to the exciting part - brainstorming and gifting!

The positive impact of corporate giving on businesses has sparked extensive discussions recently. Companies worldwide have recognized the power of corporate gifts in strengthening relationships with customers and clients, as well as establishing a more personal connection with these audiences. Consequently, more and more corporations are turning to corporate giving as a form of advertising. Below are some tried and true methods for using corporate gifts to enhance brand visibility:

We all enjoy receiving presents, don't we? Unique and thoughtful corporate gifts can strengthen the bond between companies and their clients, increase brand recognition, and even convert prospects into paying customers. Moreover, corporate gifts can serve as a source of motivation for your employees. Some of the advantages include:

1. Making employees feel appreciated: Receiving a gift from the company makes employees feel valued, which can contribute to their satisfaction and loyalty. In turn, satisfied customers are more likely to reciprocate the goodwill.

2. Promoting brand awareness and customer relationships: Nowadays, it has become a common practice for companies to celebrate special occasions like birthdays and anniversaries by giving personalized gifts to their customers. This trend has led to the rising popularity of corporate giving as a strategy for promoting brand awareness and fostering stronger customer relationships.

3. Inspiring employee loyalty and productivity: Another effective way for businesses to demonstrate appreciation for their employees is by providing them with corporate gifts. By showing care and recognition, you can inspire greater loyalty and productivity among your staff.

By leveraging corporate gifts strategically, companies can reap these benefits and create a positive impact on both their internal and external stakeholders.

Strategies for expanding your company through corporate gifts

We have previously discussed the benefits of corporate gifts for businesses. When used effectively, gifts can help build connections, enhance brand loyalty, and even expand your company. To maximize the impact of your business gift-giving initiative, consider following these guidelines:

1. Determine the most impactful gifts: Understand which gifts hold the most significance for your recipients. How can promotional giveaways benefit your company? Let's explore the practice of corporate giving and its potential to expand your business.

2. Corporate gifts as a marketing tool: In summary, corporate gifts are highly effective in spreading the word about your company and expanding your customer base. Nearly eighty percent of gift recipients expressed their willingness to do business with the company again, and over half reported having a more positive perception of the company after receiving a gift.

3. Strengthening relationships: Providing freebies to both employees and clients is an excellent way to solidify your company's position in their minds. Word-of-mouth marketing is crucial for many businesses, and giving out freebies can generate positive conversations and build trust, which is highly valuable.

4. Define your goals: Determine the purpose of buying business gifts. Do you want to express gratitude to your existing clients? Strengthen relationships with potential customers? Expand your lead pool? Whatever your objectives, employing a well-thought-out corporate gifting strategy can help you move closer to achieving them.

5. Focus on utility: To foster growth, it is advisable to provide something that is useful and practical. Choose items that will stay with the recipient long after they have used them, reinforcing your brand presence.

6. Consider timing: Selecting the right occasion for a corporate gift can be challenging. While holidays are often common choices, they may not always be the most memorable. Therefore, take advantage of opportune moments to utilize corporate gifts strategically in order to expand your business.

By adhering to these guidelines, you can leverage the power of corporate gifts to make a positive impact on your company's growth and success.

Here are some examples of when it could be appropriate to provide a business gift, including some lesser-known occasions. Remember that building a successful company goes beyond just satisfying customers; it's important to also consider your staff, as they are your most valuable asset.

1. Commemorate company milestones: Order special gifts to celebrate major achievements in the company's history.

2. Welcome and anniversary gifts for employees: Include gifts from the company in an employee's welcome basket, and honor long-serving employees with a present on their anniversary.

3. PR stunts, social media campaigns, and gifts with purchase: Gifting can be used effectively in various marketing initiatives. Mastering the art of corporate gifting can take your company to great heights!

4. Impress business associates or prospective customers: Present corporate gifts during business meetings or expos to leave a lasting impression.

5. Branding your gifts: Ensure that corporate gifts are branded. Using promotional products with your company's colors, logo, or other branding elements is an excellent way to increase brand visibility.

6. Focus on usefulness: Choose gifts that are practical and can be used regularly. The more useful the item, the higher the chances that it will be seen by more people, increasing brand exposure.

7. Budget considerations: Plan your gifting strategy with a budget in mind. Be mindful of your budget throughout the process to avoid overspending and negatively impacting your profits.

8. Consistency in gift-giving: Frequent and consistent gift-giving to employees, customers, clients, and colleagues helps keep your company top of mind. Avoid exhausting your budget on a single extravagant gift and consider spreading your resources across multiple smaller gifts.

9. Personalization: Individualize your corporate gifts whenever possible. Personalized gifts are an effective way to make a lasting impression and build client relationships.

10. Thoughtful messaging: When including a thank-you letter or message with your gift, be mindful of being inclusive and considerate. Avoid specific holiday references that may exclude or make others feel left out. Use phrases like "Happy Holidays" or "Wishing you a Wonderful New Year" to ensure inclusivity.

By considering these tips and strategies, you can maximize the impact of your corporate gifting and foster positive relationships with employees, clients, and customers.

Exactly Who Should Get a Present?

Just who are the individuals that make everything possible at your company? Your employees are vital to your success, but let's not forget about your partners, contractors, suppliers, and others in the business world. It's crucial to show appreciation to all those who contribute to your company, as it increases the likelihood of their positive impact on your business.

The great thing is that giving business presents doesn't always have to be overly expensive. With careful decision-making, you can find reasonably priced corporate gifts, especially when purchasing a large quantity of a single item.

Choosing the perfect gift can sometimes be challenging. It can be difficult to find a present that will be appreciated by all recipients of a corporate gift. In 2021, customized items were a prominent trend in the corporate giving scene, and this trend is expected to continue growing in the upcoming years.

As more employees embrace remote work, the personal touch of the office is diminished due to the prevalence of video conferencing and online meetings. As a result, businesses are seeking ways to bring back the human element to the workplace.

In this context, corporate gifts, especially customized ones, serve as valuable tools to restore that lost sense of humanity and personal connection within the business environment.

Strategic Corporate Gifting in Event Planning: A Real-World Case Study

In the dynamic world of event planning, strategic corporate gifting can play a pivotal role in enhancing the overall value proposition and potentially increasing event profitability. This case study demonstrates how thoughtful integration of gifting strategies into tiered attendance structures can create a more compelling event experience while driving revenue growth.

Foureva Media, founded by Jamar Jones, showcased the power of this approach during their inaugural "Lead the Movement Business Conference" held at the Fiserv Forum in Milwaukee. This event, designed to promote equality and inclusivity in the workforce, featured nationally renowned business leaders providing insights on marketing, brand culture, recruitment, and community involvement. The lineup included Super Bowl champion Jarrett Bush, international speaker Dr. Joe Johnson, Vanessa A. Vining of VaynerX, executive coach Justin Patton, and Marcela López Lozano, founder of Negocios Capitales.

Building on a previous successful collaboration in corporate gifting strategies, Foureva Media sought to enhance their first major conference through strategic gifting. This presented an excellent opportunity to create tiered attendance levels with exclusive benefits, enhance the value proposition of higher-tier passes, increase revenue streams from participant registrations, and demonstrate appreciation for VIP attendees.

The approach centered on implementing a tiered pass system, with VIP passes offering additional benefits and access to exclusive areas. A key component of this strategy was the creation of a VIP gift package, which included a branded, personalized "Lead The Movement" candle along with additional gifts from other promoters and sponsors. This package was designed to provide tangible value to VIP attendees, justifying the premium price point of their tickets.

To further enhance the exclusive experience, a designated VIP area was established at the Fiserv Forum, accessible only to those on the VIP list. The strategic placement of VIP gifts near the buffet area within this exclusive zone encouraged attendees to collect their gifts after lunch, ensuring high visibility and appreciation of the added value provided by their premium passes.

The execution of this strategy involved several key steps. First, a premium attendance option was designed and marketed with clear added value. The team then collaborated with sponsors to assemble a compelling VIP gift package, with the personalized "Lead The Movement" candles serving as a centerpiece gift. The exclusive VIP zone was established and clearly marked within the venue, and gifts were strategically placed for easy access and to enhance the overall VIP experience.

The results of this integrated gifting strategy were significant. The addition of the VIP pass option, enhanced by the corporate gift strategy, led to an increase in income generated from participant registrations. VIP attendees received tangible benefits for their premium investment, likely improving overall satisfaction with the event. The personalized candles served as lasting reminders of the event and Foureva Media's brand, extending the impact of the conference beyond its duration.

Moreover, including gifts from other sponsors in the VIP package provided additional value to corporate partners, strengthening business relationships. The exclusive VIP area and associated perks created a sense of exclusivity, potentially driving interest in premium passes for future events.

This case study highlights several key principles for effective integration of corporate gifting into event planning:

1. Tiered Value Proposition: Offering different levels of event passes with clear, tangible benefits can drive revenue and enhance attendee experience.

2. Strategic Partnerships: Collaborating with sponsors for gift packages can provide added value to attendees while strengthening business relationships.

3. Personalization at Scale: Branded, personalized gifts like the "Lead The Movement" candles offer a memorable touchpoint that extends beyond the event itself.

4. Location Matters: Placing gifts strategically within the event space can enhance their perceived value and ensure distribution.

5. Multi-Faceted Approach: Combining exclusive access (VIP area) with tangible gifts creates a comprehensive premium experience.

6. Brand Alignment: Choosing gifts that align with the event's theme reinforces the core message and enhances overall brand coherence.

7. Future Planning: The success of this strategy provides valuable insights for planning future events and structuring attendance tiers.

8. Measurable Impact: The increase in income streams offers a clear metric for assessing the ROI of the gifting strategy.

By thoughtfully integrating corporate gifting into their event structure, Foureva Media was able to create a more compelling value proposition for attendees, drive increased revenue, and strengthen relationships with both participants and sponsors. This real-world example illustrates how strategic gifting can be a powerful tool in event planning, enhancing the overall experience while contributing to the bottom line.

CHAPTER 7

How to Build Relationships via Corporate Gifting

Giving gifts can indeed strengthen existing bonds and help forge new connections. Corporate gifting refers to the practice of providing valuable items at business functions to establish relationships with clients and enhance existing customer relationships. The range of gifts can vary from a simple shirt to a fully paid vacation.

Remember, thoughtful and well-timed gifts can have a significant impact on both employees and customers, contributing to stronger relationships and positive outcomes for your business.

Marketing and Business Presents

Marketing a product is indeed essential for building recognition and trust in a company's offerings, ultimately leading to increased sales. The insights gained from selling more products or services can also inform future planning and improvements.

To maintain a competitive edge and enhance brand value, a company should continually introduce new items to the market. However, generating demand for these new products relies on consumers trying them and providing positive feedback to others. One effective strategy for increasing demand is distributing free samples among staff and soliciting their honest opinions. This approach allows for valuable feedback and can help generate positive reviews.

In fact, studies have shown that 43% of consumers who received free merchandise from a business were more inclined to give that company a positive review. This highlights the impact of free samples on consumer perception and the potential for positive word-of-mouth promotion.

Selecting a present for a business associate or client indeed requires careful consideration and tact to ensure the success of a marketing plan. Missteps can waste time, effort, and money. Here are some examples of gift options:

- Gift certificates for businesses
- Personalized merchandise
- Incentives for employees
- Paid vacations
- Corporate promotions

Strategic planning is crucial in the realm of corporate gift-giving, just like any other marketing campaign. It is wise to establish a budget and allocate funds appropriately, as overspending or underspending can both pose risks.

Several factors influence the amount of money allocated to corporate gifts:

1. Significance of the event: Whether it's a company tradition or a holiday party, larger budgets may be warranted for more intimate celebrations, while smaller budgets may suffice for routine holiday parties.

2. Demographics of the recipients: The number of workers or recipients influences the budget allocation. For a large number of workers, a practical solution like a candy and blanket set might be suitable. In contrast, for a smaller group of workers, such as four to five, luxury products like watches or cars may be considered, as exemplified by Tata Group at their annual corporate event in 2018.

3. Care for the recipients: The well-being and appreciation of workers, customers, and business associates should always be a top priority in corporate gift giving.

Building and maintaining strong connections with customers is a primary focus for most companies, as is increasing customer investment in the company. Corporate gifting plays a role in creating awareness and promoting products, which goes beyond traditional advertising methods.

Businesses have various ways to connect with their target audience, and corporate giving is one effective approach. Key themes related to corporate giving include:

- Maintaining publicity and corporate support
- Conducting new product demonstrations and direct sales
- Engaging in in-person advertising
- Implementing promotional sales

According to Forbes, the corporate giving industry is projected to reach $242 billion this year and is expected to continue growing at an 8.1% compound annual growth rate (CAGR) through 2024. The investment made by businesses in corporate gifts has proven to be worthwhile. Over 80% of respondents reported that gifts strengthened connections with staff and/or customers, and more than half indicated a "significant" advantage from gift giving. These advantages include making recipients feel appreciated (reported by 45%), increasing customer loyalty (43%), and improving staff retention (41%).

While giving gifts to a company is similar to giving gifts to friends and family, it's important to consider various options to choose the best gifts. The motivations and perceived benefits of corporate giving have surpassed mere financial rewards. Practical advantages like increased productivity and loyalty are overshadowed by the emotional rewards of building stronger relationships and making recipients feel appreciated. Ultimately, these factors contribute to the company's bottom line.

If you're unsure about what to get as a corporate present, consider products that provide an enjoyable and unique experience without heavily emphasizing the brand. The principle of "show, don't tell" is a valuable guideline for selecting corporate gifts in such situations. Additionally, gifts can be wrapped in the company's color scheme or feature a clever pun on the slogan, rather than prominently displaying the logo. Creating a comfortable environment for customers or clients is the first step in establishing a strong and enduring connection.

How Can Corporate Gifts Help You with Relationship Marketing?

An oft-cited saying, "To establish a long-term, successful firm, start a connection when you don't complete a sale," highlights the significance of relationship marketing in the modern corporate environment. When a company's operations are focused on satisfying customers, the business thrives. Additionally, making an effort to connect with someone pays off in the long run. Just as initiating a conversation with a stranger can lead to fruitful business outcomes, providing excellent customer service, motivating employees to their full potential, and consistently nurturing leads all contribute to increasing sales and building loyal client bases.

Business gifts are an essential component of your relationship marketing plan.

Over the years, corporate gift giving has played a critical role in not just increasing yearly sales but also:

1. Increasing the value of each consumer over time.

2. Reducing the churn rate (the percentage of employees that leave).

3. Enhancing employee loyalty and retention.

4. Creating opportunities for future cooperation or purchases.

All of this has been made possible because of the emotional connection that the presents you gave them have established, touching their hearts and fostering a sense of community with your business.

Here are five ways in which relationship marketing and corporate gift giving are complementary to one another:

1. Strengthening relationships through gift giving: Giving gifts helps establish and strengthen connections with customers, making them feel at ease and fostering a sense of belonging to your company. By incorporating gift giving into your relationship marketing plan, you can win customer loyalty and their continued business.

2. Boosting company reputation with custom presents: Personalized gifts elevate brand value and reflect your company's values, emphasizing customer connections and happiness. Thoughtful and customized gift baskets to express gratitude to loyal customers and valuable staff members can greatly enhance your company's reputation.

3. Importance of corporate gifting for business expansion: Corporate gifting holds significant importance for future business growth. Personalized presents demonstrate that you genuinely care about the recipient's

happiness, extending beyond marketing to relationship building and nurturing. Giving away free items is an effective way to increase brand awareness and leave a positive impression.

4. Achieving name recognition and positive word-of-mouth: Corporate gift giving contributes to boosting a company's name recognition through positive word-of-mouth. By gifting, you can gain a competitive advantage and attract potential customers who may also be considering your competitors. This strategy helps your company stand out and meet the needs of potential customers.

5. Demonstrating long-term commitment and customer satisfaction: Corporate gifts serve as tokens of appreciation, showcasing your long-term commitment and dedication to the best interests of your customers. Relationship marketing emphasizes adapting products and services to customer preferences, and corporate gifting is an effective way to demonstrate that you value customer relationships and prioritize their satisfaction.

By engaging customers with thoughtful and customized gifts, you can enhance customer engagement, increase customer retention, and generate positive feedback about your business. Additionally, focusing on client retention alongside attracting new customers can lead to a significant boost in revenue. Incorporating corporate gifting into your relationship marketing strategy is a valuable approach that enriches the consumer experience, encourages repeat purchases, and fosters long-term customer relationships.

So, let's discuss relationship marketing and how it can help you build strong personal connections with your customers. Relationship marketing is a branch of CRM (Customer Relationship Management) that focuses on establishing meaningful and lasting relationships with customers, leading to repeat business and loyalty.

If your goal is to foster brand loyalty based on strong personal connections, there are several strategies you can employ. Firstly, go above and beyond in your advertising efforts to make customers feel appreciated and valued. Show genuine care and interest in their needs and preferences.

Sending out gifts to existing customers can be a powerful way to enhance customer retention and strengthen brand loyalty. By selecting thoughtful and personalized gifts, you can demonstrate your appreciation for their support and make them feel special.

To provide your customers with an exceptional experience and kick-start your relationship marketing campaign, consider sending a delightful little candle or another small token of appreciation. Such gestures can leave a positive and lasting impression, creating a sense of goodwill and strengthening the customer-company bond.

Now, let's discuss the different phases of the corporate cycle and the types of gifts that are suitable for each stage.

Prospecting Gift:

During the sales prospecting stage, your team initiates the first human contact with potential new clients, which sets the foundation for future business. However, many salespeople find this phase challenging, with 40% reporting its difficulty.

At this stage, offering prospects small gifts can help establish rapport and foster more personalized interactions with your sales staff. The most effective prospecting gifts are tailored to each individual recipient and serve as a means to initiate contact before the formal sales process begins.

By thoughtfully selecting gifts throughout the prospecting period, you can lay the groundwork for a lasting connection. Customization is particularly crucial, as 96% of digital marketers believe that it strengthens their bond with customers.

Choosing the right gift to make your prospect ecstatic depends on understanding your audience, as preferences vary. Take the time to research and personalize the gifts to suit the individual recipient's tastes and interests. This personalized touch can go a long way in building a positive impression and starting the relationship on the right foot.

Client Welcome Gifts:

When leads become customers, it's important to go the extra mile and show your appreciation with a special gift. The process of onboarding a new customer can be challenging, especially if your product or service is complex. By taking the time to express your gratitude at the beginning of the business relationship, customers will feel valued beyond just their financial contribution.

You don't have to go overboard with the first gift for a new customer. A thoughtful gift basket, a box of chocolates, or a beautiful scented candle like can make a positive impact. It's crucial to customize these items for each individual consumer. Including a thank-you letter or card tucked inside is highly recommended. These gestures work together to create a fantastic first impression of your brand for the new customer.

Personal Milestones:

Building relationships is enhanced by acknowledging client milestones. By commemorating your clients' achievements, you demonstrate your interest in their personal lives beyond work. Surprising your clients with gifts for occasions such as birthdays, weddings, client anniversaries, and other significant life events is a thoughtful gesture.

When choosing gifts for significant life events, consider something that the recipient can enjoy both in and out of the workplace. This shows that you value them as more than just a business transaction. It's important to personalize the gifts based on their preferences and interests, further strengthening the connection between you and the client.

Team Milestones:

It's important to acknowledge the significant achievements your clients make in their careers. As your organization contributes to their business success, it's meaningful to recognize and celebrate their accomplishments.

By doing so, you can demonstrate how much you value your clients and their businesses.

When selecting gifts for team milestones, it's essential to consider that you'll be buying gifts for a whole group of individuals. One option is to provide embroidered hats or t-shirts featuring the logo of a major client. This allows both the customers and their staff to proudly display your brand while celebrating their team's achievements in the workplace. It serves as a reminder of the successful partnership and the positive impact your organization has had on their business.

Corporate Holiday Gifts:

Gift-giving is a cherished tradition during the holiday season. Including customers in your gifting budget is a great way to express gratitude for their business and foster a personal connection that can strengthen long-term relationships. By giving presents to people during the holidays, you show that they are still valued despite the busyness of the season.

When selecting gifts for employees during the Christmas season, it's beneficial to choose items that have practical use outside of the workplace. Providing client appreciation in the form of a home accessory is a win-win situation. Not only will it be useful in their personal lives, but it will also leave a positive impression of your business and the connection they have with you beyond the workplace. This aligns with the essence of relationship marketing, as you want people to perceive you as both a friend and a professional partner. By nurturing this bond, you can establish loyal patronage and lasting relationships with your customers.

Client Check-In Gifts:

These gifts, which I like to refer to as "just because" presents, are given without any specific reason or occasion. In fact, "just because" gifts can often be the most heartfelt and appreciated gestures. They show that expressing gratitude to your clients is not limited to a particular event, but rather a genuine and ongoing sentiment. These gifts demonstrate that you care about your clients and that your organization is always there for them whenever they need it. By surprising them with a thoughtful gift when they least expect it, you strengthen the bond between your business and your clients, fostering a sense of loyalty and trust.

Loyalty Rewards Programs:

Strengthening customer loyalty and enhancing your connection with them can be achieved quickly and easily by implementing a loyalty rewards program. Research has shown that such programs can increase client retention by 5%.

As mentioned earlier, loyalty points hold significant power as a customer retention tool. However, it is important to note that different models of loyalty reward programs exist, and not all of them are suitable for every company. These programs work particularly well for companies with shorter sales cycles, as customers may feel overwhelmed by the idea of accumulating rewards points over an extended period.

In the case of shorter sales cycles, a points system can be implemented to reward customers for their purchases. For instance, reaching a specific point total could earn them a shop gift card. By implementing this type of loyalty incentives program, both client retention and revenue can be increased.

Alternatively, another approach is to offer a high-value prize once customers reach a certain sales threshold. This not only demonstrates your appreciation for their patronage but also encourages repeat business from them, strengthening the bond between your company and its loyal customers.

Customer Support Gifts:

Sometimes, the sales process encounters hiccups and clients may become frustrated. In such situations, offering customer support gifts can be a great way to address the issue and show your support. These gifts serve as a gesture of goodwill and can help mend the relationship. Consider a basket of tasty treats as a thoughtful present that is always appreciated in such circumstances.

Delighting and retaining customers is entirely possible through relationship marketing. Building personal connections and being personable with customers lies at the core of relationship marketing. That's why offering freebies and gifts plays a crucial role in boosting satisfaction and loyalty among existing customers.

Showing gratitude to your closest people in life often involves giving gifts, and the same principle applies to recognizing and rewarding loyal customers and fostering strong connections with them. Taking the time to surprise and please your customers with thoughtful presents can generate profit and keep them happy. Providing exceptional service and treating customers as individuals is all that's required.

Customer acquisition and retention through personal connections are often overlooked aspects of business. Communication with customers after regular business hours should be treated no differently than during the day. This implies that marketers need to emphasize providing a customized and individual experience to successfully cultivate B2B partnerships. By taking the time to know clients on a personal level, businesses are more likely to win them over as customers.

In today's business environment, corporate giving is one of the most effective and crucial strategies for marketers, sales representatives, or business development professionals to establish meaningful interactions with prospects and customers they want to do business with. Giving someone a gift is a way to treat them as a person rather than a commodity, whether they are an employee or a representative of the company.

A corporate gift is given in a business environment, distinguishing it from a personal present given on special occasions like birthdays. While each gift has its own unique purpose, they all ultimately serve the same goal. Offering a gift can be a great way to initiate a conversation with a new contact or strengthen relationships with existing ones. Corporations use gifts as a means to solidify connections with customers, partners, and employees.

In the context of the pandemic, when in-person interactions are limited, effective communication has become even more important. A thoughtful and customized gift can be a powerful way to express appreciation and strengthen relationships with others.

Personalizing a gift for the recipient contributes to highly successful experiences and enhances the connection with the recipient.

In today's marketing landscape, there is a significant amount of competition for the attention of your target audience through various media commercials and email campaigns. Many commercial email campaigns end up in crowded inboxes, and primetime media commercials may lead your target demographic to switch channels and avoid promotional content.

As a result, a considerable portion of your marketing budget may go to waste, which is a common occurrence even for experienced teams. To address this, it is worth considering innovative methods to capture customers' attention.

Including corporate gifts in your marketing mix is a solid strategy that can significantly improve the return on investment (ROI) of your advertising budget. Well-planned corporate gifts have the potential to make your marketing efforts stand out in a world dominated by constant digital stimulation. While it is impossible to completely ignore the digital environment in today's technology-driven culture, corporate gifts can complement your digital marketing efforts.

Let me explain how you can make an impact.

Building rapport with top-level executives, who often hold decision-making power in businesses, can be challenging.

Gifting your client-facing employees with promotional items featuring your company's brand and marketing message can help alleviate any awkwardness that may arise during interactions with potential new customers. It helps customers remember your company and the executive who presented to them. Providing appropriate promotional products to your company's top executives can greatly facilitate your sales team in breaking the ice and establishing client connections, which can lead to significant returns for your firm.

Corporate gift-giving is a strategic approach that can significantly influence your brand's visibility and customer loyalty. By offering personalized and branded items, businesses can create positive experiences for their clients and employees, which helps to establish a strong and memorable brand image. These gestures foster goodwill and appreciation, making recipients more likely to advocate for your brand through word of mouth.

This approach not only strengthens relationships with existing customers by making them feel valued and appreciated but also aids in attracting new clients through positive referrals. Engaging with your customer base through thoughtful gifts can lead to enhanced customer loyalty, and in cases where there may have been past issues, can help repair and improve those relationships.

Moreover, corporate gifts can be an effective way to boost employee morale, promote a positive work environment, and encourage staff to act as brand ambassadors. Happy employees often provide better customer service, which can further enhance the company's reputation and lead to better business outcomes.

Using Corporate Gifts for Brand Recognition and Consumer Loyalty

In today's competitive market, especially within the realms of business and digital marketing, grabbing and maintaining attention is critical. Attention is a scarce resource that can significantly impact a company's success. Building strong brand recognition is essential, influencing virtually every business operation. It stands as a paramount goal for companies aiming to establish a presence in their industry.

However, attracting attention is a double-edged sword. Not all attention will be positive, and navigating this landscape can be challenging for any business. Efforts to stand out might not always resonate positively with a target audience, potentially complicating the path to a favorable reputation. But when a company is recognized for genuinely benefiting its customers and community, it can lead to a significant influx of new clients. A well-regarded company that treats its clients, employees, and customers with respect often attracts both new and repeat business.

Corporate gift-giving emerges as a strategic tool in this context. Across all levels of the corporate ladder, the value of a well-considered gift remains undeniable. Gift-giving fosters stronger relationships, creating a foundation of trust and camaraderie. It's more than just the exchange of items—it's a demonstration of appreciation and goodwill. This practice can be particularly effective in building a loyal consumer base. When companies consistently show appreciation through gifts, whether to clients during the holiday season, or to employees as a recognition of their hard work, it reinforces a positive image of the company.

Moreover, corporate gifts serve multiple functions—they can be a token of gratitude, a marketing tool, or a means to make amends. Every gift sent out into the world carries the potential to bring back a positive return, whether in the form of strengthened relationships, enhanced company reputation, or direct business outcomes. By thoughtfully integrating corporate gift-giving into their marketing strategies, companies can create lasting impressions that contribute to sustained business success.

Through this approach, businesses can not only retain their existing customer base but also attract new clients who value a company that cares about its stakeholders. The practice of giving can set a business apart in a crowded marketplace, transforming every corporate gift into an investment in the company's future.

The success of corporate gift giving can be attributed to its practicality. People rarely anticipate presents, which is why they are so effective in building relationships and trust. Gift giving is a wonderful way to show customers how much you appreciate them and their business. Taking it a step further by adding a personalized gift and a heartfelt message expressing gratitude for their support can elevate the experience.

Publicly displaying appreciation and offering small gifts can go a long way in showing employees that their efforts are valued at work. Additionally, corporate giving can lead to increased sales through word-of-mouth advertising.

When launching a new business, there are numerous obstacles to overcome. How can you become well-known in a fresh market? How can you expand your clientele? Corporate gift giving is a strategy that often gets overlooked but can help address these challenges. By giving corporate presents on special occasions, you can show appreciation to the people who contribute to the success of your company. When executed effectively, it can enhance overall productivity and set your company on the path to success.

Expanding your business into a new consumer base can be daunting. Keep in mind that you may have a limited customer base, a scarcity of suppliers and prospects, and a limited financial foundation. Establishing your name and achieving early success with your product is crucial for building a solid foundation for future growth. Corporate gift giving, which can be seamlessly integrated into your company's model, is a valuable strategy for overcoming this obstacle.

Corporate gift giving makes it easier to create a memorable impression on prospective customers. Providing a small token of appreciation as a follow-up or after the initial meeting with a customer can have a significant impact on how others perceive your business and you personally.

Customers who remain loyal over time are not only financially beneficial but also serve as powerful brand advocates. Research has shown that customers will continue to return if the process is straightforward and rewarding, despite efforts from competitors. Fair pricing and high-quality products or services align with customers' expectations. A company's ability to retain its clients depends on how well it appreciates their loyalty and addresses any issues that may arise promptly. Remember, showing appreciation, whether to long-time customers or those who made significant purchases, is essential and will not be forgotten.

Moving on, there's another crucial concept to explore that can shift your perspective on building corporate relationships and the idea of gifting. It's time to delve into what we refer to as **Return on Kindness**.

What Is Return on Kindness?

Although it is still important to track over time, measuring "return on kindness" (ROK) is an underappreciated statistic that can help companies succeed daily. In a world that still faces strife and turmoil, every business can provide a safe haven for workers to come together and pursue a shared purpose. By fostering positivity and loyalty, businesses can guarantee long-term success.

Creating a negative working environment with derogatory comments, flippant comebacks, a lack of cultural awareness, and disrespect for others' sentiments hinders a company's success. People often become defensive in conversations because they feel judged instead of receiving different perspectives. Acting kindly and positively prevents retaliation and keeps lines of communication open, which is crucial for rapidly expanding businesses.

Now, you might be wondering, "What's the big deal about return on kindness?"

Being compassionate does not imply a lack of strength, especially for powerful company entrepreneurs. The term "kin" in "kindness" signifies a connection between individuals or a network of people. The industry recognizes that compassion in the workplace is impossible without a sense of community. Strong personal relationships among staff members lead to greater commitment to their employers. Knowing that they contribute to a greater whole and work towards a shared goal is inspiring.

A company that values its workers, clients, and suppliers will thrive. Experts emphasize the importance of recognizing the value of one's work within the context of a larger group or team. Patience is essential for maintaining solid connections between individuals, especially in a society where multitasking is the norm.

Industry experts advise being generous with thanks, praises, and recognition for everyone in the company, even for the smallest contributions. Personalized gratitude from business owners or management to customers makes a noticeable impact.

The ability to genuinely connect with employees and customers is crucial for a leader's goals, business, and corporate culture. Corporate gifts provide an opportunity to demonstrate concern and empathy, fostering genuine connections.

The Importance of Personalization: A Real-World Case Study in Holiday Appreciation Gifting

In the realm of corporate gifting, holiday seasons present a unique opportunity to strengthen client relationships and set the stage for future business growth. This case study demonstrates how a well-executed holiday gifting strategy can combine personalization at scale with thoughtful presentation to create lasting impressions and drive business success.

Shay Rowbottom, a prominent figure in social media marketing and coaching, recognized the potential of holiday gifting to show appreciation to her clients and generate excitement for the upcoming year's services. Building upon previous successful collaborations in corporate gifting, we developed a strategy that would not only express gratitude but also reinforce Shay's brand and pave the way for continued business relationships.

Our approach centered on leveraging and enhancing a previously successful strategy: branded candles with QR code technology. The key innovation in this campaign was the integration of personalized video messages. When clients scanned the QR code on their candle, they were directed to a video where Shay personally thanked them, extended holiday wishes, and shared New Year greetings. This combination of a physical gift with a digital, personalized message created a multi-sensory experience that resonated deeply with recipients.

The campaign's execution was a testament to the power of personalization at scale. Despite reaching clients across five different countries, each gift felt uniquely tailored. The process involved careful preparation of customized labels, generation of unique QR codes, and meticulous packing and shipping coordination. This attention to detail ensured that each client, regardless of their location, received a high-quality, personalized gift that reflected Shay's appreciation for their business.

The results of this holiday gifting campaign were overwhelmingly positive. Shay received numerous emails from clients expressing their appreciation for both the gifts and the personalized video messages. This feedback provided tangible evidence of the campaign's success in strengthening client relationships. Moreover, the branded candles served as lasting reminders of Shay's services, subtly reinforcing her brand long after the holiday season had passed.

Perhaps most importantly, the gifts helped generate excitement for continued coaching services in the upcoming year. By timing the gifting campaign with the holiday season, Shay not only tapped into the cultural expectation of gift-giving but also positioned her brand at the forefront of clients' minds as they planned for the new year.

This case study highlights several key principles of effective corporate gifting:

1. Leverage technology for personalization: The use of QR codes to deliver personalized video messages allowed for a scalable yet deeply personal approach to gifting.

2. Build on past successes: By iterating on a previously successful strategy, we were able to enhance the impact while minimizing risk.

3. Balance scalability and personal touch: Despite the campaign's large scale, spanning multiple countries, each client felt personally acknowledged through the video message.

4. Time your gifting strategically: Utilizing the holiday season aligned with cultural expectations and heightened the emotional impact of the gesture.

5. Ensure consistency in brand experience: The branded candles provided a tangible, long-lasting reminder of Shay's brand, complementing her digital presence.

6. Use gifts to build anticipation: The holiday gifts served not just as a thank you, but also as a subtle reminder of Shay's services for the upcoming year.

7. Consider global implications: Successfully executing an international gifting campaign highlighted the importance of logistical planning in corporate gifting strategies.

8. Measure impact: The email responses from clients provided direct feedback on the campaign's success, offering valuable insights for future gifting strategies.

This real-world example illustrates how thoughtful, strategic corporate gifting can transcend the act of giving a simple present. When executed with care and consideration, a gifting campaign can become a powerful tool for strengthening client relationships, reinforcing brand identity, and driving business growth. By combining the warmth of personal appreciation with the efficiency of scalable solutions, businesses can create memorable experiences that resonate with clients long after the holiday season has passed.

CHAPTER 8

Winning Strategies For Your Corporate Gifting

We have explored numerous gifting ideas so far, covering topics such as corporate relationships and the importance of gifting. By now, I'm confident that you understand the significance of corporate gifting and how it can contribute to the growth and success of your business and relationships.

Now, let's talk about some practical tips for developing a winning gift-giving plan.

To reap the benefits of gift giving, you need a well-defined strategy with concrete steps for giving to customers, staff, and potential new business. Without a solid plan, it will be challenging to make significant progress in the corporate world, so conducting thorough research is crucial.

Your plan should consider factors like the allocated budget for presents, preferred brands, the number of gifts to be given, the recipients, and the delivery method. Determine who should receive a gift and establish appropriate timing for contacting them and presenting the gift.

Start by familiarizing yourself with the norms and practices of corporate gift giving in your customers' companies. Understand if it is customary for them to exchange presents and tailor your gifts accordingly based on the level of business and value they bring to your organization. Personalization and unique corporate gifts should be reserved for the most valuable customers.

Tips for Developing a Profitable Corporate Giving Plan

What's not to like about adding direct mail and gifts to your Account Based Marketing strategy? Giving gifts can be a terrific method to gain access to new accounts and strengthen existing connections. Our findings indicate that giving has a net positive effect on our sales funnel. However, to maximize the direct mail channel's ability to build demand, you'll need a gifting plan that aligns with the rest of your advertising efforts. Creating a successful gifting strategy that guarantees B2B demand generation involves several moving parts. If you want to succeed, follow these solid guidelines and keep them in mind:

The Key to Successful Corporate Giving is Personalization

You should always make an effort to provide each potential client with the corporate present they deserve. Take some time to reflect and offer gifts that are tailored to the recipient's unique interests and aspirations. The more thought and effort you put into a present, the greater the impact will be. Therefore, it is crucial to be attentive to the cues and individual insights that your prospects share with you. Pay close attention and inquire about information that sets you apart from the competition. Engage in discussions about their weekend activities and their preferences. For example, if you know they'll be spending a Friday night alone at home and would appreciate a takeout meal, consider sending them a

Deliveroo certificate. These small gestures demonstrate that you value the person and genuinely care about them.

To capture potential customers' attention, try surprising them with a personalized bottle of champagne or a birthday gift. In fact, this embodies the essence of Account-Based Marketing. Personalized and thoughtful gifts have the potential to expedite the sales process and even lead to larger contracts.

Make Use of a Gifting System With Tiers

Do you recall our previous discussion on this topic? The significance of a tiered approach cannot be overlooked, which is why I want to emphasize it again. Each potential client is unique, so customize your approach to align with their industry experience and level of influence. Since not all prospects are the same, it's crucial to consider the types of gifts that different levels of seniority would appreciate. Corporate gifting campaigns aimed at C-suite contacts should be structured differently than those targeting lower-level connections.

Having a well-defined ideal customer profile has been proven to increase account win rates by 68%. Therefore, it is essential to prioritize higher-quality leads by offering them more valuable gifts and creating personas for your ideal customers.

If you apply the same principle to your budgeting, you will observe positive outcomes. Your gifting strategy should be tailored based on the account's value: high-value or enterprise accounts require individualized attention, while lower-value accounts can receive gifts in bulk.

Always Remember to Let the Sales Cycle's Phases Serve as a Guide

To select the optimal corporate gift for each individual lead or client, it is important to take into account their position in the buying process.

If you have had only a few interactions with a prospect and have limited knowledge about them, it might be preferable to begin with a more general offer, such as an e-voucher for coffee and a request to speak with a sales development representative. However, if they are a recurring client who has previously engaged with your company's account executives, you have more flexibility to be imaginative.

Initiate a Gesture of Reciprocity but Don't Count on Receiving Anything in Return

The key is to give freely to others without expecting reciprocation.

Prospecting is an art form. However, just because you've invested effort (and expense) in creating a unique gift for a promising lead doesn't mean it's exactly what they need at the moment. Since scheduling meetings consistently can be challenging, it's important to adopt a mindset of giving without expecting anything in return.

Take advantage of upcoming holidays to align your approach with the broader context.

It's a proven strategy to offer gifts to potential clients and existing clients during the holiday season. If you want to simplify your offering and increase the chances of arranging that initial meeting, it's a wise decision to tie gifts to national observances like International Coffee Day and Earth Day.

For example, for International Coffee Day, you could provide potential customers with a coffee making kit along with a custom cup. Alternatively, for a more straightforward option, you could give them a gift card to pick up a cup of coffee on their way to work. Consider celebrating Candle Day with some delightful scented candles as well. The key is to ensure that your company remains on their minds during these significant dates.

Look for less conventional celebrations to base your corporate gifting campaigns around, as they tend to capture more attention. By offering presents to potential customers and partners during unexpected times of the year, you can surprise and delight them. Explore our selection of candles for your holiday gifting campaigns targeting leads, customers, and staff.

Make Sure Your Gifting Approach is in Step With Your Sales Rhythm

Establishing a consistent sales rhythm is an effective strategy for keeping your company top of mind for potential customers. By aligning your sales cadence with your gifting approach, you can enhance the effectiveness of both.

Strategic gift mailings to relevant prospects and customers can be integrated between cold email and cold call sequences. Including a freebie in your offer is an excellent way to differentiate yourself from competitors and increase the likelihood of closing the deal.

In fact, when a gift is included, our closing rate experiences a remarkable 100% boost. Impressive, isn't it?

To ensure smooth operations, it's also advisable to synchronize your sales cadence with your broader marketing strategy, as well as any upcoming campaigns and events for your business.

Have a Party to Celebrate Successes With Clients and Customers

Corporate gift giving has been proven to enhance renewal rates among existing customers. It's a wonderful way to demonstrate your appreciation for their business by sending champagne on the anniversary of your collaboration. Even when facing potential customer attrition, this strategy can serve as a reminder of the value you bring to the table.

Research across various fields has consistently shown the power of giving tokens of appreciation to inspire gratitude and loyalty in clients, colleagues, and other business associates. However, it's crucial that the gifts themselves are appropriate; nobody needs yet another branded stress ball.

Regularly expressing gratitude to your customers and clients should not be underestimated, although it may seem obvious, it is often overlooked.

When it comes to the challenge of finding gifts of the right size, there are several options available. One approach is to incorporate your company's values and culture into the gifts, thereby fostering brand loyalty and employee engagement. Now, I will share what I have discovered.

Let's talk about timing: In my line of work, it is customary to start working on projects with long lead times, such as proposing Christmas-themed ideas in July. It's like stepping into another world, imagining snow and the festive atmosphere while dealing with sweltering temperatures and thoughts of beach getaways. However, it's inevitable, just like giving presents is a natural part of life. Planning and preparing for company holiday gifts need to be done well in advance to ensure they are completed in time for the holidays.

To overcome this challenge, make it a habit to prepare ahead of time. This way, you'll have ample time to get everything right. Remember, rushing through the process often leads to mistakes and hiccups, which is something you can't afford when dealing with something as delicate as corporate gifting.

The fourth quarter is a busy time of year, and sourcing gifts requires effort. It's crucial to avoid giving poorly thought-out presents that will be immediately noticeable. To ensure this doesn't happen, it's best to conceive and implement an effective gift-giving strategy well in advance.

When it comes to buying and packing holiday gifts, experts recommend completing these tasks by the end of October. Why is it necessary to start working so far ahead? Well, the holidays and the end of the year are notorious for causing shipment delays due to increased volume. It has become a tale as old as time!

Every year, we encounter delays during the holiday season. The overwhelming demand leads to supply constraints, so it's important to prioritize securing access to the components essential for implementing your plan. (Early indications suggest that the pandemic's impact on supply chains may potentially affect sourcing and threaten shipment timetables throughout the holidays.)

Collecting all the addresses for a large gift send may take three weeks or more, unless you have a streamlined process in place.

When it comes to the month of December, professionals recommend sending out shipments in the first or second week. People you're trying to reach are likely still at home before they leave for the holidays. Additionally, consider giving presents to your clients at other times of the year. This is an excellent strategy for standing out and maintaining brand recognition ahead of a potentially fruitful period.

Narrating a tale is important when giving gifts. It's not just about giving something to show you care; it's about having a plan for what you're giving and what it represents. Create a narrative with the presents you provide that highlights the relationship between the recipient and your business. Traditional swag presents that people simply throw away are a waste of money.

Before you even begin the process, it's essential to have a well-defined goal for the narrative you want to convey. To stimulate your thinking, consider the following questions:

- Why are you doing this?
- What story do you plan on telling?
- What types of presents do you think would best convey that story?

With these considerations in mind, you can develop an idea that is both beneficial to your target audience and representative of your brand.

A company wanted to give its employees a unique gift. The delivery included items such as Twinkies, honey, and whiskey goblets. The message sent along with the gift was bright and concise, reflecting the organization's values and providing a moment of joy for the recipients.

Another way to demonstrate your company's commitment to diversity, equity, and inclusion is by purchasing from small companies owned by minorities or women.

When offering gift choices, it's important to provide options without overwhelming the recipients. If your budget is limited, you can give them a choice between several gifts. This approach is particularly useful for distributed teams. As a rule of thumb, aim for one gift choice per 200 recipients, with a total of three or four options. Categorize each choice into groups such as cuisine, cocktails, outdoor/adventure, family activities, or workplace necessities. Ensure that the cost of each choice is comparable to prevent automatic selection based on price.

Regardless of the gift choice, always remember to include a kind message. Add a personal touch by writing a warm and empathetic message that aligns with the overall plan and narrative you're conveying. While handwritten notes are preferable, if you need to send a large number of messages quickly, a video message sent via QR code can be a fun and surprising alternative. You can include a QR code that allows recipients to access a video of your CEO expressing gratitude or providing context for the gift.

Consider adding modest branding, such as a letter, to the package without detracting from the overall aesthetic.

Lastly, don't overlook the excitement of opening the package. Make sure the packaging is appealing and adds to the anticipation and thrill of receiving the gift.

The care and attention put into the presentation of a gift reflects the sender's appreciation, and the gift is not complete until the recipient sees what they have received.

When considering the unpacking experience, it's important to focus not only on the visual aspects but also on how other senses can be engaged. For example, some companies have proposed including a QR code on the outside of Christmas packages that leads to a video of a crackling fire, allowing the recipient to enjoy the sound of a fire in the background while opening the gift. This creative approach adds an extra touch of brilliance to the experience.

While the idea behind a gift is important, it's the intentional preparation and consideration that truly demonstrates appreciation for the recipient. Inspired by everything I've discovered, I've started planning my Christmas presents, and I hope you feel the same way.

In today's fast-paced world, where face-to-face interactions are increasingly rare, it's crucial to invest time and energy into establishing and maintaining meaningful connections with clients, customers, sales prospects, and employees. Symbolic tokens in the form of gifts have gained popularity as companies shift away from large-scale events. With the limitations of video conferencing, more businesses are turning to gift-giving as a novel way to express gratitude, attract new customers, and increase brand recognition.

Corporate giving plays a role in customer retention, which, in turn, boosts profits and aids in sales prospecting. When done strategically and at the right moment, gift-giving can be an invaluable tool for advancing professional goals. Gift-receiving is an emotional event that fosters a sense of closeness and bonding.

To maximize the return on investment from corporate gifts in your upcoming campaign, consider the following emerging trends:

Business Gift Sets with Personalized Gift Boxes

In 2021, there was a notable increase in the demand for branded gift boxes, customized business presents, and swag packs.

The growing prevalence of virtual meetings, remote teams, hybrid workforces, and other forms of remote work is a trend that continues to gain momentum. As a result, corporate gifts have become even more impactful. Whether your goal is to impress potential customers, reward dedicated employees, or achieve both, this guide can assist your business in delivering thoughtful and memorable corporate gifts.

Packaging and Presents Made from Sustainable Materials

Sustainable products and environmentally conscious companies are gaining popularity among American consumers. There is a growing interest in eco-friendly and sustainable corporate gifting, and there are several ideas on how to continue offering fantastic gifts in 2022 without exceeding your budget. Lucky Penny Candles, for instance, were made from eco-friendly and renewable materials, ensuring they won't end up in a landfill after just a few years.

The Gift of Discretion

Choice-based giving, aligned with sustainability, has emerged as a rapidly growing trend driven by technological advancements. By offering individuals the freedom to choose gifts that resonate with their interests and needs, you can make a lasting impression while streamlining your gift-giving process. Providing employees with the option to select their own holiday and work anniversary presents through digital codes sent via email, SMS, digital gift cards, or QR codes is an excellent way to express appreciation. Gifting based on recipient preferences can not only help your company save money but also reduce waste.

Crafted Items from Your Neighborhood

In 2021, there was a significant surge in the popularity of gifting gourmet foods and other specialty items sourced regionally or locally. Best-selling gift baskets predominantly featured products either made in the United States or crafted by local artisans and merchants. There is a growing demand among younger customers for locally produced, organic, and artisanal food gifts. These presents offer a straightforward yet impactful way to make a positive impression in 2022.

Highlighting Important Occasions

Corporate giving is expected to be influenced by the ongoing pandemic, leading to a shift in gifting strategies. Rather than focusing primarily on holidays, future trends will emphasize specific events and anniversaries throughout the year. Building and strengthening relationships with employees, clients, and customers will be a continuous effort to enhance brand recognition. In the coming years, maximizing the return on investment in corporate gifts will be a key focus.

To optimize your company's gift-giving budget, experts suggest outsourcing a significant portion of your corporate gift operations. This can help save both money and manpower. Sustainable business gifts during the holiday season are an excellent way to foster connections with colleagues, clients, and customers. Meaningful and personalized corporate gifts can boost morale and show appreciation to individuals or entire teams during this busy time.

While it may seem challenging to shop for a large team with varying preferences and dietary restrictions, proper preparation and expert guidance can make the process straightforward and stress-free. Here are some key pieces of advice for corporate gift-giving:

First, Make a List of Everyone You Want to Contact and Get Their Addresses

Having a well-organized list of all the gift recipients is the first step to ensuring a smooth transaction. Take into consideration whether they are currently remote workers or in-office employees. If a significant portion of your staff is still working remotely, make sure to obtain their residential addresses so that you can deliver eco-friendly gift boxes to their homes. Take note of these details and begin the process promptly to stay on schedule.

Please Deliver Your Gifts Early

This point cannot be emphasized enough, and that's why it deserves a prominent place in your corporate gifting strategy. I understand how busy things can get during the holiday season, so I urge you to submit your orders as early as possible. The period from the 1st to the 17th of December is typically when the highest volume of gift basket orders is received. To avoid any disappointment or shipping delays, please make your purchases as soon as possible.

An additional advantage of delivering presents early is that the recipients will have more time to enjoy and savor them.

Create a Budget

Before diving into any brainstorming or research for your corporate gifting campaign, it's crucial to establish and approve a budget. This budget should cover all related expenses, including branding and shipping costs. Having a clear budget is very important because it helps you plan and carry out your campaign effectively, ensuring everything goes smoothly and achieves the expected results.

To aid in this financial planning, consider using a budget worksheet. What if you had a tool that team members could fill out or refer to during the planning process? This worksheet could be incredibly helpful, providing a structured way to manage costs and keep your campaign within financial limits. By laying out all expenses in a budget worksheet, you can avoid surprises and make informed decisions about where and how to allocate funds, making your corporate gifting campaign more efficient and impactful.

Include a Heartfelt Note for the Recipient

Including a handwritten message of appreciation or congratulations is a thoughtful gesture that can significantly enhance the impact of your company present. It shows that you have taken the time and effort to personalize the gift and acknowledge the recipient's specific contributions or achievements. By being specific in your message, you demonstrate genuine appreciation for your team's efforts and help boost their motivation. A handwritten note adds a personal touch that conveys your gratitude in a more heartfelt manner, making a lasting impact on the recipient.

Act With Conscience and Appropriateness

Giving business gifts is intended to strengthen relationships and foster goodwill. It is important to consider the preferences and needs of the recipients, including factors such as their religion, dietary restrictions, and health. By taking these aspects into account, you increase the likelihood that the gifts will be well-received and appreciated.

For example, if you are sending a gift to a vegan coworker, it would be thoughtful to customize the contents of the gift to align with their dietary preferences. You may consider exploring vegan gift baskets, which are specifically designed to cater to individuals following a vegan lifestyle. These baskets can offer a selection of vegan-friendly products that your coworker will truly enjoy and appreciate.

Focus on the Values of Your Company

It is wonderful to express appreciation to your staff through corporate gifts, but what if those gifts could also make a positive impact in the world? In today's business landscape, where businesses are under increased scrutiny, it is important to plan how to effectively showcase your company's commitment to ethics and the environment.

Our corporate gifts not only allow you to reach out to your employees and customers, but also contribute to important environmental and social initiatives. By selecting gifts that align with your company's values, you can create personal connections and foster a loyal and engaged community of satisfied customers.

Gifts have the power to demonstrate your appreciation for new customers and leave a lasting impression of your company's professionalism. According to YouGov, 62% of high-spending consumers consider emotional ties with a brand as a key factor in their continued loyalty. Even in a competitive market, a thoughtful token like a holiday gift can make new customers feel confident in their choice to engage with your business. By providing gifts that are both in line with your brand and reflect the needs of the recipients, your company stands out as a caring organization.

By selecting corporate gifts that represent your company's values and contribute to positive change, you can make a meaningful impact while strengthening your relationships with employees, customers, and the community at large.

It's time to reintroduce your business to the market and remind your clients of your value. Promoting the fact that you have something new and exciting to offer, such as a redesigned website, updated branding, or revolutionary product, can help maintain a positive relationship with your clientele. Sending gifts along with significant news is a great way to inform colleagues about new opportunities to collaborate and remind satisfied customers of their positive past experiences.

Showing appreciation to loyal customers, whose feedback and opinions have guided your new company strategy, through gifts of appreciation is a wonderful way to express gratitude and make a rebrand or relaunch worthwhile. When customers feel personally involved and valued by your business, they are more likely to recommend your products or services to others and be willing to participate in testing new products and techniques. Remember that a genuine gesture of gratitude or a delightful surprise for regular customers can significantly strengthen your relationship with them.

When sending care packages, it's important to go beyond a simple "thank you." Gift-giving is about genuinely caring for one another as individuals and expressing that care. Even after completing a project or professional engagement, it's crucial to continue nurturing relationships. Look for opportunities to send unexpected yet appreciated care packages to key individuals in your network, especially those with whom you have spent a significant amount of time. Maintaining and cultivating these connections is increasingly important, as studies show that up to 68% of companies lose customers when they perceive the company as indifferent.

Sincere displays of concern are always welcomed, whether it's sending a care package to a loyal client who just had a baby or gifting a bottle of wine to a busy business associate who has recently moved. These gestures of thoughtfulness help strengthen relationships and foster a sense of genuine care and appreciation.

Thoughtfully designed referral gifts that reward customer loyalty and encourage new customers to engage with your business can significantly enhance your community presence when expressing gratitude. Customers who refer your company to others should feel like valued members of your family and be acknowledged with a token of appreciation. Furthermore, empowered customers appreciate this connection as it validates the importance of their relationship with your brand. This bond evolves into a mutually beneficial collaboration for both parties.

Regardless of how innovative your product or service may be, it will not have a meaningful impact on your customers' lives or contribute to your company's growth unless you establish genuine connections with them first. If you want to add a personal touch to your interactions with customers and clients, consider incorporating well-thought-out corporate gifts into your strategy. Additionally, consider trying out corporate candles as a unique gift option.

Creative Engagement Through Corporate Gifting: A Case Study from BITCON 2022

In the fast-paced world of technology conferences, standing out and making meaningful connections can be challenging. This case study demonstrates how creative thinking in corporate gifting can enhance engagement and create lasting impressions, even in unexpected contexts.

At BITCON 2022, an annual conference hosted by the Blacks In Technology Foundation at Walt Disney World in Orlando, Jamar Jones, founder and CEO of Foureva Media, showcased the power of innovative corporate gifting. As a keynote speaker discussing diversity, equity, and inclusion in the technology sector, Jones faced the challenge of engaging a diverse audience of IT professionals, university students, and afro-technologists.

Building on previous successful experiences, Jones and his team developed a strategy that went beyond traditional conference swag. They chose to use branded Lucky Penny Candles as their primary engagement tool. This decision to offer a tangible, non-tech gift at a technology conference was a bold move that paid off in multiple ways.

The approach centered on creating a system where attendees could fill out a form to receive their free candle after Jones' speeches. This strategy served dual purposes: it provided a tangible thank-you gift to attendees and created an opportunity to collect valuable contact information for future networking and marketing efforts. Moreover, Jones personally distributed the candles, allowing for direct interaction with attendees beyond his keynote address.

The execution of this strategy involved careful planning. Jones crafted his keynote to incorporate mentions of the upcoming gift opportunity, creating anticipation among the audience. The candles were branded specifically for the event, likely incorporating elements related to technology and diversity. A dedicated area was established near the speaking venue for candle distribution and form collection, ensuring a smooth process for attendees.

The results of this creative gifting approach were remarkable. Attendees noted the novelty of receiving candles at a tech conference, which immediately set Jones apart from other speakers. The candles served as effective conversation starters, facilitating networking opportunities in a natural and engaging way. Jones received numerous compliments on this innovative approach to audience engagement, demonstrating the strategy's success in creating a memorable experience.

Perhaps most importantly, the branded candles served as long-lasting reminders of Jones' message and the conference, extending the impact of his presentation well beyond the event itself. The distribution process allowed for additional face-to-face interactions with attendees, further solidifying connections made during the keynote address.

This case study highlights several key principles for effective corporate gifting in conference settings:

1. Unexpected gifts create memorability: In a tech-focused environment, tangible, non-tech gifts like candles can stand out and be memorable.

2. Engagement beyond the speech: A well-planned gifting strategy can extend the impact of a presentation, creating additional touchpoints with attendees.

3. Dual-purpose strategies are effective: The approach served both as a thank you to attendees and as a data collection opportunity.

4. Personal distribution adds value: Having the speaker personally involved in gift distribution enhances the perceived value of the interaction.

5. Cross-industry appeal is possible: The success of this strategy at a tech conference demonstrates the versatility of thoughtful corporate gifting.

6. Brand reinforcement is key: Branded gifts serve to reinforce both personal and corporate messages.

By thinking creatively about engagement tools and corporate gifting, Jones was able to create more meaningful interactions with conference attendees. This approach not only enhanced his personal brand but also provided tangible benefits in terms of networking opportunities and data collection. The success of this strategy at a technology conference under-scores the potential for innovative corporate gifting to make a significant impact in various professional settings.

CHAPTER 9

Gifting Strategies for Promotional Events

A thoughtful gift is always well-received. It's rare to find someone who would refuse something they desire when it's offered for free. Therefore, it's not surprising that giving is one of the most powerful techniques available to marketers.

When we examine the process of giving, it becomes clear why it works as a form of marketing. The giver anticipates and fulfills the recipient's needs with a gift. The recipient appreciates and utilizes the gift, which leads to a sense of gratitude towards the giver. As a result, the recipient develops positive feelings towards the provider.

In essence, by giving the right gifts to the right people, you can have a remarkable impact on your company's reputation. When you provide something valuable to your audience, they will be more often willing to give you their time and attention.

At promotional events, capturing attention is half the battle, and free gifts help businesses achieve that. Incorporating gift-giving into your marketing strategy at promotional events can help you reach more people and increase awareness.

Recipients respond positively to corporate gifts because, like personal gifts, they are thoughtfully selected. However, in corporate giving, the gift itself is never the primary message but rather a tangible asset that helps convey it.

By strategically offering corporate gifts at promotional events, businesses can achieve hyper-efficient marketing that attracts new visitors to their booth.

Ensure that your event is memorable by offering attendees a token that will leave a lasting impression on their minds.

Corporate gifting is a delicate balance. The gift should not only attract people to the event but also create a lasting impression that encourages ongoing engagement.

Gifts are an excellent way to maintain excitement and promote a message long after the event has ended. However, they should not feel like cheap afterthoughts but rather serve as permanent mementos.

A thoughtful, unique gift is more appreciated than a disposable trinket that will end up collecting dust on someone's desk or in the trash. Since you invest a significant amount of money to bring people to business events, it's important not to skimp on mementos that they will cherish.

Distributing free items at events is a great way to enhance people's familiarity with your brand and prompt them to consider making a purchase from you.

It's remarkable how much impact a small gesture can have. As we've witnessed in life, even the smallest acts can go a long way. So make sure to choose the right promotional gift, as 83% of buyers say they are more likely to buy from a company that has provided them with a freebie.

What's the Best Way to Promote Your Presents?

In the dynamic landscape of corporate events, crafting a comprehensive gifting strategy can transform a mere gesture into a powerful engagement tool. Each strategy below offers insights into maximizing the impact of corporate gifting, ensuring that your brand leaves an indelible mark on event attendees.

Thematic Alignment

Aligning your gift selection with the event's theme or purpose creates a cohesive experience that resonates with attendees.

For instance, at a technology summit, consider providing gadgets or tech accessories that mirror the event's focus. This alignment underscores your brand's understanding of the event's context and adds value to both the gift and the event itself.

Personalization

If you've made it this far into the book, you probably understand how big of a deal personalization is. Personalized gifts elevate the experience for attendees, demonstrating a level of thoughtfulness that makes recipients feel valued.

Incorporate personal touches such as engraved names, custom messages, or tailored variations of the gift based on attendees' preferences. This strategy fosters a sense of individual recognition and connection to your brand.

Interactive Giveaways

Create interactive moments that lead to gift rewards. Incorporate trivia quizzes, scavenger hunts, or social media challenges that encourage attendees to actively participate. These activities not only generate excitement but also provide opportunities for attendees to engage with your brand in a fun and memorable way.

Surprise and Delight Moments

Incorporate surprise elements into your gifting strategy to evoke positive emotions and stand out in attendees' memories. Randomly distribute gifts throughout the event or host surprise reveals to keep attendees engaged and eager to see what's next. These unexpected moments can create lasting impressions and amplify the event's enjoyment.

Digital Engagement

Extend your gifting strategy into the digital realm by offering valuable digital gifts. Provide exclusive access to webinars, e-books, or online courses that align with the event's theme. Digital gifts not only cater to a tech-savvy audience but also provide lasting value, extending beyond the event's duration.

Value-Added Partnerships

Leverage partnerships with other brands or vendors to enrich your gift offerings. Collaborative gifts that combine your products or services with those of partners enhance the perceived value of your gifts. This approach also enables cross-promotion, reaching new audiences and expanding your brand's presence.

Social Media Amplification

Harness the power of social media by creating a dedicated event hashtag and encouraging attendees to share their experiences with your gifts. Highlight user-generated content on your brand's social platforms to foster a sense of community and engagement. This amplification not only increases brand visibility but also encourages attendee participation.

Post-Event Follow-Up

Maintain momentum after the event by sending follow-up emails or messages to express gratitude for attendees' participation. Include additional resources, such as event highlights or bonus content, as part of the follow-up. This ongoing engagement reinforces the positive impression created during the event and extends your brand's influence.

VIP Treatment

Identify key attendees, loyal customers, or high-value clients, and offer them premium gifts that reflect their significance to your brand. Tailoring gifts to their preferences and recognizing their importance can foster stronger relationships and encourage advocacy for your brand.

Exclusive Previews

Generate excitement by offering exclusive sneak peeks or pre-sales of upcoming products or services as part of your gift package. By providing attendees with a glimpse into your brand's future offerings, you create a sense of anticipation and engagement that extends beyond the event.

Thoughtful Packaging

Elevate the presentation of your gifts by incorporating creative and thoughtful packaging. The packaging itself communicates your brand's attention to detail and enhances the perceived value of the gift. Well-designed packaging creates an immersive unboxing experience that resonates with attendees.

Sustainability Focus

Eco-friendliness and sustainability matter a lot to people. Demonstrate your commitment to sustainability by offering eco-friendly gifts or integrating sustainable practices into your gift distribution process. Sustainable gifts align with the values of environmentally conscious attendees and contribute to your brand's reputation as a responsible corporate citizen.

Feedback Loop

Encourage attendee feedback by including a mechanism for sharing thoughts and opinions about the event alongside your gifts. This feedback loop not only provides valuable insights for refining future events but also fosters a sense of inclusion and investment among attendees.

By implementing these nuanced strategies, you can transform your corporate gifting approach into a holistic engagement strategy. Remember that the effectiveness of these strategies lies in their seamless integration with your brand's identity, the event's objectives, and the preferences of your target audience.

Here Are Some Things You Should Try

In the ever-evolving landscape of corporate events, the art of gifting continues to evolve, presenting exciting opportunities to engage attendees and leave a lasting impact. To ensure your brand stands out, here are some innovative corporate gifting strategies to explore:

Set Up a Contest on a Social Media Platform

Social media is undoubtedly one of the most accessible platforms on mobile devices, playing a significant role in forming connections and nurturing partnerships. Organizing a contest where the winner receives one of your new promotional items is an excellent strategy to engage with your customers and generate excitement for your upcoming event. By using catchy taglines and clever hashtags, you can generate interest and boost attendance by offering guests an opportunity to win free promotional items.

Distribute Free Products at Your Next Event

The most effective strategy for creating lasting brand recognition beyond the event day is to distribute merchandise. Customers love freebies, and when event attendees proudly display your swag such as T-shirts, tote bags, notebooks, water bottles, and travel mugs, it serves as a powerful endorsement of your company and ensures ongoing visibility.

Event attendees share the goal of expanding their professional networks, so providing them with an opportunity to showcase their support for the event through these freebies strengthens your brand's relationship with its target audience. It's important to consider the needs of your target demographic and what you want them to remember when they see your offerings.

Business Cards

Distributing business cards at events is a reliable way to ensure that potential customers have convenient access to your contact information at all times. Since networking is a key objective at events, it's important to equip yourself with appropriate event swag. Choose a visually appealing business card design that effectively conveys essential information about your company and features a catchy headline.

Ensure that your company name, contact number, email address, and any other important details are prominently displayed. Consider using Business Card Holders to make your contact details stand out even more.

Another delightful option is to provide customers with an Edible Logo that showcases your contact details. Include a QR code on the packaging that directs consumers to the information gathering page on your website. QR codes can work wonders, which is why we're talking about them again. This tasty approach not only attracts more customers but also helps you grow your contact list.

Achieve Maximum Impact

Instead of trying to cater to the diverse preferences of every event attendee, consider using items with bold colors and captivating designs to attract attention to your booth. Whether it's a custom water bottle or a fun tote bag, provide them with something practical that they can use during the event and remember you by.

This swag will not only help to create brand recognition among potential customers but also make your booth stand out among competitors who are also vying to increase their company's visibility, generate leads, and close sales.

We are now in the era of corporate events, and the aforementioned suggestions are just the beginning. There are countless opportunities to choose from that can ensure the success of your next promotional event.

Interactive Tech Experiences

Embrace the digital age by incorporating interactive technology into your gifting strategy. Consider providing attendees with virtual reality experiences or AR-enabled products that showcase your brand's offerings in an immersive and memorable way. These tech-driven gifts not only intrigue attendees but also position your brand as forward-thinking and tech-savvy.

Personalized Gift Workshops

Take the personalization trend a step further by offering on-site workshops where attendees can customize their own gifts. For example, you could set up a station where attendees design their own T-shirts. Offer various stencils, fabric paints, and plain T-shirts, and let each person create their own design that reflects their style or mood.

Another great workshop idea is a jewelry-making session. Provide all the necessary supplies like beads, clasps, and strings in a variety of colors and materials. Participants can mix and match to craft their own bracelets or necklaces. This not only lets them express their creativity but also gives them a lovely accessory to remember the event by.

For those who enjoy home decor, consider a workshop for creating personalized candles. Supply different scents, colors, and jars, and teach attendees how to mix these elements to create custom scented candles. This kind of workshop not only offers a fun activity but also results in a beautiful, functional piece that can add a personal touch to any room.

These workshops not only make your event more interactive and enjoyable but also ensure that everyone leaves with something special that they've made themselves, enhancing their connection to the experience.

Wellness and Self-Care Kits:

Incorporate well-being into your gifting strategy by providing attendees with wellness and self-care kits. Include items such as aromatherapy products, relaxation tools, and healthy snacks. These thoughtful gifts prioritize attendees' health and comfort, leaving a positive and lasting impression on their event experience.

Digital Gift Cards with a Twist

Elevate the traditional gift card by infusing creativity and customization. Offer digital gift cards that allow recipients to select their preferred brand or product from a curated list. This strategy not only provides flexibility but also enhances the element of choice, making the gift more meaningful and tailored to individual preferences.

Brand Storytelling Through Gifts

Transform your gifts into storytellers by infusing them with your brand's narrative. Create a series of gifts that collectively tell a story, unveiling different aspects of your brand's journey, values, and offerings. Each gift becomes a chapter, and as attendees receive them, they become immersed in your brand's unique tale.

Interactive QR Code Experiences

Utilize QR codes to create interactive experiences tied to your gifts. Attendees can scan the code to access exclusive content, behind-the-scenes videos, or interactive games. This strategy adds an element of surprise and exploration to your gifts, enhancing attendee engagement and interaction.

Trend-Conscious Gifts

Stay attuned to current trends and cultural shifts to curate gifts that resonate with attendees' interests. Whether it's eco-friendly products, wellness essentials, or tech gadgets, align your gifts with what's capturing the collective attention. Trend-conscious gifts showcase your brand's relevance and ability to connect with attendees on a cultural level.

Mystery Box Unveiling

Generate excitement and anticipation by presenting attendees with mystery boxes. These boxes contain surprise gifts that attendees unveil during the event. The element of surprise creates a memorable and suspenseful experience, and attendees leave with not just a gift but also a sense of adventure.

Collaborative Art Installations

Elevate your gifting strategy by involving attendees in collaborative art installations. Provide a canvas or interactive art piece where attendees can contribute their own artistic touch. This creative approach not only engages participants but also results in a tangible artwork that serves as a lasting memory of the event.

Virtual Gift Lounges

Incorporate the virtual aspect by creating online gift lounges where attendees can explore and choose their preferred gifts. This approach provides attendees with flexibility and convenience while still offering a curated selection of items that resonate with your brand.

As you navigate the realm of corporate gifting, these strategies open doors to innovative and engaging experiences. By embracing these cutting-edge approaches, you can foster deeper connections, elevate your brand's presence, and create truly unforgettable event experiences.

The Importance of Personalization: A Real-World Case Study in Tradeshow Gifting

In the fast-paced world of tradeshows and expos, standing out from the crowd is crucial for attracting potential clients and making lasting connections. This real-world case study demonstrates how strategic corporate gifting can be effectively adapted to a tradeshow environment, combining immediate rewards with long-term marketing potential to maximize client attraction and engagement.

On October 6th, 2022, the "Delta 8 Expo" was held in Orlando, Florida. Shay Rowbottom, a prominent figure in social media marketing, was scheduled as a panel speaker to discuss the importance of authenticity in social media promotional messaging. This event presented an ideal opportunity to showcase the power of personalized corporate gifting in a high-energy, competitive environment.

Building on the success of a previous event sponsorship for Shay Rowbottom earlier that year, we developed a multi-faceted gifting strategy aimed at expanding reach, encouraging booth visits, and growing Shay's email list for future marketing opportunities. The approach we crafted demonstrates the versatility and effectiveness of personalized gifting in a tradeshow setting.

Our strategy centered on a two-pronged gifting approach that balanced immediate gratification with a high-value incentive. We offered branded candles as free gifts to all visitors, providing an instant reward for stopping by the booth. Additionally, we featured a Vibration Plate Exercise Machine as a sweepstakes prize, creating a compelling reason for attendees to engage further with Shay's brand.

To streamline the engagement process and leverage technology, we incorporated a QR code on the candle labels. This innovative touch allowed participants to quickly access a specific online form, sign up for Shay's email newsletter, and enter the sweepstakes to win the Vibration Plate Exercise Machine. By combining physical gifts with digital interaction, we created a seamless experience that appealed to the tech-savvy audience at the expo.

The execution of our strategy was carefully planned to maximize visibility and engagement. We secured a strategic booth placement near the main stage, ensuring high foot traffic. The display prominently featured both the candles and the Vibration Plate Exercise Machine, creating an eye-catching presentation that drew attention from across the expo floor. The streamlined process allowed visitors to scan the QR code, receive their free candle, and enter the sweepstakes in a matter of seconds, minimizing barriers to participation.

The results of this personalized gifting strategy were immediately apparent. The unique combination of immediate gifts and a high-value sweepstakes prize drew significant attention to Shay's booth, increasing overall traffic and engagement. Many attendees were unfamiliar with the

Vibration Plate Exercise Machine, which provided an excellent opportunity for Shay's team to engage in meaningful conversations about its benefits and functionality, deepening connections with potential clients.

The free candles served as an effective icebreaker, encouraging more people to interact with the booth and creating a positive first impression of Shay's brand. By incentivizing email list sign-ups, Shay's team collected valuable contact information for future marketing efforts, extending the impact of the expo far beyond the event itself.

This case study highlights several key takeaways for effective corporate gifting at tradeshows. First, the dual incentive strategy of offering both immediate gifts and a chance to win a high-value item appealed to different motivations, maximizing engagement across a diverse audience. The use of QR code technology simplified the sign-up process, reducing barriers to participation and increasing the number of leads collected.

Choosing a unique, lesser-known item as the main prize created natural opportunities for conversation and product education, allowing Shay's team to showcase their expertise and build rapport with potential clients. The use of branded candles with QR codes demonstrated how personalization can be achieved at scale, maintaining a personal touch while efficiently collecting data from numerous attendees.

Perhaps most importantly, this strategy balanced immediate benefits to attendees with long-term value for Shay's business. While providing instant gratification through free candles, the focus on building an email list ensured sustained marketing opportunities beyond the event. This approach showcases how strategic corporate gifting can be adapted to create lasting impressions and drive business growth, even in the fast-paced and often overwhelming environment of a tradeshow.

By learning from and building upon the success of previous events, we were able to refine and improve our gifting strategy, demonstrating the importance of continuous innovation and adaptation in corporate gifting practices. This real-world example illustrates how personalized, strategic gifting can be a powerful tool for attracting clients, fostering engagement, and creating long-term marketing opportunities in a competitive business environment.

CHAPTER 10

Tying Everything Together

As we conclude our journey through "The Corporate Gifting Playbook," let's revisit the transformative power of strategic gifting in the business world. Throughout this book, we've explored how thoughtful corporate gifts can be a catalyst for building meaningful connections, fostering loyalty, and driving business growth. From showing gratitude to employees and clients, to leveraging gifts for brand recognition and customer engagement, we've seen how a well-executed gifting strategy can set your business apart in today's competitive landscape.

The key to successful corporate gifting lies in its personalization and strategic implementation. We've learned the importance of choosing the right gifts, understanding the dos and don'ts of business gift-giving, and recognizing the crucial role of timing and context. Whether you're an entrepreneur looking to strengthen relationships, a marketing professional aiming to enhance brand loyalty, an HR specialist focusing on employee retention, or a sales professional seeking to close deals, the strategies outlined in this book provide a roadmap for turning corporate gifting from a routine practice into a powerful business tool.

Remember, the true essence of corporate gifting goes beyond the material value of the gift itself. It's about creating a culture of appreciation, trust, and mutual respect. As demonstrated through our real-world case studies, when done with genuine intention and strategic thought, corporate gifting can yield surprising results, fostering long-lasting relationships and driving tangible business success. As you move forward with your gifting strategies, always keep in mind that the heart of gifting lies in making others feel valued and appreciated. By doing so, you'll not only achieve your business objectives but also create a positive impact that extends far beyond the bottom line.

For those eager to dive even deeper, full versions of the case studies presented throughout this book are available on our companion website: www.GiftingPlaybook.com. But that's not all – the website also hosts a treasure trove of additional resources, including gifting strategy blueprints to help you prepare for your next corporate gifting event. These tools are designed to help you immediately apply the knowledge gained from this book, turning insights into action.

As you embark on your journey to harness the power of strategic corporate gifting, remember that continuous learning and adaptation are key. The resources on our website will be regularly updated to reflect the latest trends and best practices in corporate gifting. We encourage you to visit often, share your own experiences, and be part of a growing community of professionals who understand the transformative power of thoughtful, strategic gifting.

Thank you for joining me on this exploration of corporate gifting. I'm confident that with the strategies, insights, and resources provided in this book and on our website, you're well-equipped to elevate your business relationships and drive success through the art of strategic gifting. Here's to your future gifting endeavors – may they be personal, impactful, and tremendously successful!

A Lesson in Kindness: The Hawaii Special Education Story

As we conclude our journey through the world of strategic corporate gifting, I want to share a personal story that embodies the true spirit of what we've explored in this book. This experience not only reinforced the power of thoughtful gifting but also reminded me of the profound impact we can have when we extend our gifting strategies beyond the traditional business realm.

In September 2022, as the founder of Lucky Penny Candles, I found myself reflecting on my past as a college instructor. The challenges faced by educators during the COVID-19 pandemic weighed heavily on my mind. It was then that a conversation with my friend Amber Weber, a Certified Occupational Therapy Assistant in Hawaii's Leeward District, sparked an idea that would bring our gifting principles full circle.

Amber shared stories of the extraordinary efforts made by special education staff in Hawaii. These dedicated professionals had gone above and beyond during the pandemic, often working in challenging conditions to ensure their students received the care and education they needed. Their stories of resilience and commitment touched me deeply, and I knew I had to act.

Drawing on the strategies we've discussed throughout this book, I reached out to Jody Agpalsa, the District Education Specialist of the Pearl City/Waipahu complex. My proposal was simple yet meaningful: to gift our Lucky Penny Candles to the special education staff as a token of appreciation for their tireless efforts.

The process of preparing and sending these gifts to Hawaii was more than just a logistical exercise. It was a moment of reflection on how the principles of strategic gifting could be applied to create genuine, heartfelt connections. Each candle represented not just a product, but a beacon of gratitude and recognition for these often-overlooked heroes of education.

As I coordinated this gifting initiative, I was reminded of the key lessons we've explored in this book:

1. The power of personalization: By choosing gifts that resonated with the recipients' experiences, we created a more meaningful connection.

2. The importance of timing: Recognizing their efforts in the wake of the pandemic added significance to our gesture.

3. The impact of unexpected appreciation: By reaching out to a group not typically targeted for corporate gifts, we amplified the emotional resonance of our action.

While I didn't receive direct feedback from the recipients, the act of giving itself was profoundly rewarding. It served as a powerful reminder that the strategies and principles we've discussed throughout this book have applications far beyond driving business growth or closing deals. They can be used to spread kindness, boost morale, and create positive change in our communities.

As you move forward with your own gifting strategies, I encourage you to look beyond the immediate business benefits. Consider how you can use these principles to make a difference in your community, to recognize unsung heroes, or to simply spread joy where it's needed most.

Remember, at its core, strategic gifting is about human connection. It's about making others feel valued, appreciated, and seen. Whether you're nurturing a client relationship, motivating your team, or thanking community heroes, the fundamental principle remains the same: give with intention, give with heart.

As we close this book, I hope you'll take this story as an inspiration. Let it remind you that the strategies we've explored are not just business tools, but powerful ways to create positive change in the world. May your future gifting endeavors be not only successful but also deeply meaningful, leaving a lasting impact on both your business and your community.

Thank you for joining me on this journey. Here's to a future where strategic gifting becomes a force for kindness, appreciation, and positive change in the business world and beyond.

References

[1] HR Morning. "The power of kindness in the workplace." https://www.hrmorning.com/articles/kindness/

[2] Stanford Graduate School of Business. "The Psychology of Kindness in the Workplace." https://www.gsb.stanford.edu/insights/psychology-kindness-workplace

[3] National Institutes of Health. [Study title or brief description]. [Year if available].

[4] Tamberino, E. (2024, February 12). How Giving Can Fill Your Heart & Increase Longevity. Vail Health. https://www.vailhealth.org/news/how-giving-can-fill-your-heart-increase-longevity

[5] The Advertising Specialty Institute®. (n.d.). Study on promotional gift brand recall. Retrieved from www.asicentral.com (membership required for access)

[6] Obvi. A/B Test on Subscription Service Gift Offering.

[7] Motista. (2018, September 27). New Retail Study Shows Marketers Under-Leverage Emotional Connection. PR Newswire. https://www.prnewswire.com/news-releases/new-retail-study-shows-marketers-under-leverage-emotional-connection-300720049.html

[8] British Promotional Merchandise Association (BPMA). (n.d.). Study on the impact of corporate gifts. Retrieved from https://www.bpma.co.uk

Index

About the Author

Image credit: Christine Nicole Photography

Dom LeRoux is a strategic corporate gifting expert and the author of "The Corporate Gifting Playbook." Born and raised in Montreal, Canada, Dom developed a deep appreciation for personalized gifts in his childhood, often purchasing meaningful mementos on family trips to Niagara Falls. This early fascination with thoughtful gifting laid the foundation for his future endeavors.

Driven by a passion for personal and professional growth, Dom pursued higher education in the United States, earning a degree from Bellevue University and furthering his studies in e-commerce and business at Northcentral University. His career has spanned collaborations with renowned companies in the consumer packaged goods and on-demand printing sectors, providing him with valuable industry insights.

Dom's innovative approach to corporate gifting culminated in a year-long experiment where he created "Lucky Penny Candles," a line of premium scented candles. He gifted these candles to business owners across the United States and Canada, meticulously documenting the impact and results of his strategic gifting practices. This hands-on experience forms the backbone of "The Corporate Gifting Playbook," offering readers real-world strategies for leveraging corporate gifts to drive business growth, foster customer loyalty, and boost employee engagement.

As an advocate for personal growth, positivity, and gratitude, Dom applies these principles to both his professional and personal life. He serves as a member of the Advisory Panel for the Digital Marketing Certificate Program at The University of South Florida Muma College of Business, contributing his expertise to shape the next generation of marketing professionals.

Dom's unique blend of childhood experiences, academic background, professional achievements, and innovative gifting experiments position him as a leading voice in the field of strategic corporate gifting. Through "The Corporate Gifting Playbook," he shares his insights and strategies, empowering businesses of all sizes to harness the power of thoughtful gifting for organizational success.

The History and Meaning of Lucky Penny Candles

Dom LeRoux, the author of "The Corporate Gifting Playbook," explores the power of strategic corporate gifting to fuel business growth. Over the course of a dedicated year, Dom personally provided his innovative "Lucky Penny Candles" to numerous business owners across the US and Canada. This hands-on approach allowed him to observe firsthand the impact of thoughtful gifting on attracting new customers, retaining existing ones, and fostering talent retention.

Dom's book covers real-life examples and measurable results derived from these experiences. By expressing gratitude to employees as a talent retention tactic, approaching prospective customers at local events, and showing appreciation to loyal clients, Dom's strategies benefit businesses of all sizes—from solopreneurs to large corporations. His insights apply across various departments such as HR, Sales, and Marketing, helping them achieve their goals through effective gifting practices.

What truly sets this book apart is Dom LeRoux's unparalleled dedication. Unlike the common approach of resorting to generic, impersonal swag items, Dom invested considerable time and effort into creating and distributing the "Lucky Penny Candles" as a way to innovate and refine his gifting strategies. His book offers a refreshing perspective on leveraging strategic gifting to drive business success.

Whether you're looking to enhance employee morale, increase customer loyalty, or stand out in a competitive market, "The Corporate Gifting Playbook" provides the insights and tools necessary to harness the power of thoughtful, impactful gifting.

Dom LeRoux's extensive research and practical experience make this a must-read for anyone serious about using gifting as a strategic business tool.

Book Dom to Speak at Your Next Event!

Dom LeRoux is deeply passionate about empowering businesses to excel in client retention, new account acquisition, and employee satisfaction through the strategic use of corporate gifts. This unwavering drive and dedication have fueled Dom's extensive research and hands-on experience in the field of strategic gifting, positioning him as a leading expert in this innovative approach to business growth.

With years of experience as a seasoned business development professional and successful entrepreneur, Dom has amassed a wealth of knowledge that he eagerly shares with others. His expertise spans across various industries and business sizes, making him a versatile and invaluable speaker for a wide range of events.

Dom is available as a Keynote Speaker or Guest Presenter for:

- HR conventions and events focusing on employee retention and satisfaction
- Marketing and sales tradeshows seeking innovative customer acquisition strategies
- Private corporate events exploring unique approaches to talent and client retention
- Business conferences looking for fresh perspectives on relationship-building in the corporate world

Known for his engaging speaking style and practical, actionable advice, Dom thrives on connecting with his audience and providing valuable insights.He takes great pleasure in imparting his expertise, drawing from his own experiences and proven strategies to help business owners and professionals expand their horizons and flourish in their respective fields.

To invite Dom to speak at your next event or to learn more about his consulting services in strategic corporate gifting, please visit www.Dom-LeRoux.com. Discover how Dom's unique approach to corporate gifting can transform your business relationships and drive sustainable growth.

www.ingramcontent.com/pod-product-compliance
Lightning Source LLC
Chambersburg PA
CBHW071603210326
41597CB00019B/3387